DOMINION WITHIN

Dominion Within

Rev. Glen A. Kratzer

The Bookmark
Santa Clarita, California

Copyright 2003 by Ann Beals

All rights reserved under the International
and Pan-American Copyright Convention

Library of Congress Control Number: 2003103948

Kratzner, Glen.
    Dominion within / by Glen Kratzer.
    p. cm.
    ISBN 0-930227-50-6

1. Christian Science. 2. Spiritual healing.
3. Prayer. I. Title.

Published by
The Bookmark
Post Office Box 801143
Santa Clarita, California 91380

To
My Faithful Wife

To whom, under God, I was indebted for healing through Christian Science treatment from apparently incurable disease, and through whom I received much of my education in Christian Science, this book is lovingly dedicated.

The Author

MRS. EDDY'S DEFINITION
of
"Authorized Literature"

The following is quoted from Article VIII, Section 11, of the *Church Manual of the First Church of Christ, Scientist, in Boston, Massassachusetts*:
"A member of this Church shall neither buy, sell, nor circulate Christian Science literature which is not correct in its statement of the divine Principle and rules and the demonstration of Christian Science. Also the spirit in which the writer has written his literature shall be definitely considered. His writings must show strict adherence to the Golden Rule, or his literature shall not be adjudged Christian Science." Written by Mrs. Eddy.
Each person has a right to judge for himself as to whether any book, pamphlet or article measures up to this test.

PREFACE

In 1907, the author wrote an article for a distant patient, and entitled it "Dominion Within." This article was published in the *Christian Science Sentinel* of February 19th, 1908. Two days thereafter, the author received from Rev. Mary Baker Eddy an autograph letter, now in his possession, the first sentence of which is: "Your article, 'Dominion Within,' is superb"; and this article met with wide commendation from the field of Christian Science students and workers. It is reproduced as the first article of this book, it having been long out of print.

Since the article appeared, the author has had five years of additional experience in the practice of Christian Science and in developing his understanding of God, as manifest in the human consciousness, along lines similar to those touched upon in "Dominion Within"; and all of the articles in this book deal with the application of Christian Science to human needs. They are offered to the public in the hope that they may be found useful by those who are struggling to gain that practical knowledge of God which will enable them to gain the victory over sin, disease, and other forms of human ill.

In this book, a very few lines of thought and practice are treated and illustrated in a large variety of ways. If there be a noticeable sameness in the points dwelt upon in various articles, let it be remembered that the purpose of the book is not to furnish entertainment to the casual reader, but to help the earnest student of Christian Science work out the most serious life problems which confront him. Every article is true to the leading thought indicated by the title of the book, that *dominion is within*.

TABLE OF CONTENTS

Dominion Within ... 1

Getting Rich ... 4

Divine Love Meets All Needs ... 11

The Law of Right Feeling ... 14

The Consciousness That Heals ... 20

Prayer ...24

From Sickness to Health ... 32

Working in Truth ... 39

Hindrances to Healing ... 43

Trusting God ... 51

Rejoicing in Tribulation ... 55

The Righteousness Which Is by Faith ... 62

Dealing with Malpractice ... 68

God-Consciousness versus Sub-Consciousness ... 73

God the Rewarder ... 79

The Marriage of Truth and Love ... 83

Let Your Conversation Be in Heaven ... 85

"Perfect Love Casteth Out Fear" ... 89

Working Out Our Problem ... 92

The Urge of God ... 98

Work for the Patient ... 101

Self-Surrender through Love ... 105

Making the Port ... 113

Is God Our Father-Mother? ... 115

The Lame Walk ... 118

TEXTS FOR THE BOOK

Whom shall he teach knowledge? And whom shall he make to understand doctrine? Them that are weaned from the milk. For precept must be upon precept, precept upon precept, line upon line, line upon line.
Isaiah 28: 9, 10

Let the word have free course and be glorified. The people clamor to leave cradle and swaddling clothes. Truth cannot be stereotyped; it unfoldeth forever.
Mary Baker Eddy
No and Yes

A few books, which are based on this book [*Science and Health*], are useful.
Mrs. Eddy
Science and Health

By loyalty in students, I mean this: Allegiance to God, subordination of the human to the divine, steadfast justice, and strict adherence to divine Truth and Love.
>
> Mrs. Eddy
> *Retrospection and Introspection*

Everyone should build on his own foundation, subject to the one builder and maker, God.
>
> Mrs. Eddy
> *Retrospection and Introspection*

He that hath an ear, let him hear what the Spirit saith unto the churches. To him that overcometh will I give to eat of the tree of life, which is in the midst of the paradise of God.
>
> Revelation 2:7

DOMINION WITHIN

He that ruleth his own spirit is better than he that taketh a city.
Adapted from Prov. 16:32.

Christian Science teaches that God is infinite Person, infinite individuality; that He is the unbounded consciousness. In *Science and Health with Key to the Scriptures* Mary Baker Eddy writes, "God is infinite, the only Life, substance, Spirit, or Soul, the only intelligence of the universe, including man." It is well for us to spend a portion of our time in trying to rise into some sense of that unbounded consciousness, that sense of freedom from limitation whereby we may endeavor to know God in His wholeness; but the endeavor to become conscious of God in His infinity, is usually not the best means of realizing those present and particular manifestations of Him which we need to realize in order to meet certain problems that confront us.

God is ever-present good; and He is manifested in specific good, as well as in general good. Often what we need to realize are those specific manifestations of good which, in our limited state of belief, we are more readily able to comprehend. For example, if we seem to be threatened with a lack of money to meet our needs, or with lack of supply of any kind, or with disaster in business, and the thought of this is troubling us, we should stand still where we are, or retire to our closet, and "have it out" with the one evil then and there, or just as soon as possible, by knowing and declaring that the ever-present law of God, good, the ever-present fact for the children of God, is plentiful supply.

The truth is that as plenty is man's birthright, plenty is the present fact for those who accept the truth; and error, false sense, cannot make us believe to the contrary. If we realize this fact long enough and clearly enough, so that it becomes vital to us, we shall have entered into peace and joy, and error will no longer argue fear to us. If, even by a single moment's realization of the truth, we have permanently healed our consciousness — cast out fear, and brought in the abiding sense of security and joy — our outward affairs will take care of themselves in due season. We do not need, beyond ordinary prudence and common sense, to trouble ourselves about the external arrangement or disposition of material things, or to be anxious about negotiations with our fellow-men. Our one problem is to maintain a whole consciousness, devoid of fear, resting in God as the abundant and infallible source of supply; then the outward things will be added unto us.

Christian Science also teaches us to know that health, strength, sight, and hearing, or any other special manifestation of God, good, from which we may seem to be cut off, are present and unchangeable facts of our true selfhood, and that error cannot make us believe to the contrary, or make us fear the further seeming loss of any of these manifestations of good. If we heal our own consciousness, so that we have no further sense of fear, but are able to rest with a sense of security and joy in the fact that the special manifestation of good which we desire is a present and indestructible fact, that is all we need to be concerned about. The physical manifestation will duly take care of itself, and harmony will be realized where before discord was apparent. It was never more than an appearance; for God, the sole creator, never made any discord, but rather established harmony as the eternal law and the eternal fact; and so it is. At the creation, "God said, Let there be light; and there was light;" and the light (the good) remains to this day, while its opposite, darkness, in reality does not exist.

We should not be anxious for the morrow or about any outward things — either supplies for daily need or health of the body; but we should seek first the kingdom of God, which is "at hand" and "within you," and His righteousness (right thinking and feeling, knowledge of the truth, and love devoid of fear), and all these outward things will be added unto us. We should be willing to be "absent from the body" in thought; we should not worry about it, nor try to cure it by taking thought about it. We should not try to control the body by our thought; we should try only to control our consciousness by meditating on God and His law. Thus we shall be "present with the Lord," and the body will soon manifest harmony.

* * * * * * *

Whatever of health or wealth we gain apart from conscious reliance upon God while we are gaining them, is worthless.

GETTING RICH

At the beginning of our earthly experience, as soon as we are old enough to enter into conscious life, we begin to seek after material things. A child discovers that he gets satisfaction from food, pets, clothing and toys. As he grows older, he still seeks after material things, but the nature of his wants and demands gradually changes. However, in time he discovers that he does not get as much satisfaction out of these material goods as he formerly did, even if he is able to gain most of the things which he desires, which is seldom the case. Nevertheless, there are unnumbered thousands of people upon whom it never seems to dawn that there is any other order of riches to be sought for; and so, notwithstanding the failure of material possessions and pursuits to give desired satisfaction and happiness, great numbers of people continue, from the cradle to the grave, a mad race to gain them, and never consciously enter into higher realms of life which are always at hand for them, if they only knew how to enter in.

A careful analysis will be instructive. All that the houses, public buildings, banks, and stores filled with merchandise in any city, can even seem to confer upon the people of that city are comfort and satisfaction. But comfort and satisfaction are states of consciousness, and not phenomena of matter. Were it not for the presence of consciousness, all the material things in a city would have no more significance than a dust heap, for consciousness alone can appreciate or set a value upon them. A peck of diamonds is worth nothing to a horse, and a peck of corn is worth nothing to a stone. Accordingly, it is easy to see that material riches have no value, except insofar as they can be made the means of increasing the riches of consciousness. So it is apparent that fundamental riches are desirable states of consciousness, and that material goods are riches only in a secondary sense. To realize this, and govern our activities accordingly, is great gain. "Set your affections on the things which are above; not on things on the earth."

If the average man had a thousand dollars in his possession, and knew that there was a decided liability that burglars would try to break into his house at night, he would take great precaution to guard that treasure. He would either place the money in the bank, or else he would equip his doors and windows with burglar alarms, and possibly arm himself, prepared to fight, if necessary, to guard his treasure. This he would do, because he consciously set a distinct value upon the money. But how many people are there who will guard their mental treasure-house, their consciousness, with equal care? How many people consciously place such a value upon peace and joy and love, that they will guard against being despoiled of them even more carefully than they would guard against being despoiled of material treasures? If they awake to the fact that these desirable states of consciousness constitute fundamental riches, then they value them even more than they value material goods, and guard them with corresponding care. But most people hold peace, joy, and love at so small a valuation that they will allow even a trifling circumstance to invade their consciousness and steal away these treasures, leaving in place of them anger, envy, jealousy, anxiety, grief, and other afflictive mental states.

Some gossip comes along with a tale that a friend has said some unkind or unjust thing. Promptly, without even waiting to learn whether the tale is true, the listener allows peace, love and joy to be taken out of his consciousness. The loss of property, the sickness of a friend or relative, an insulting word, a pain in the body, and a dozen other outward occurrences are allowed to effect the same result. These things are often permitted to enter our mental treasure-house and steal away our jewels without protest or objection. This is never the case, however, if we learn that desirable states of consciousness are the true riches, and that they are more worth keeping a secure hold upon than any amount of material goods. Then we will be at great pains not to allow outward occurrences to interfere with our true, inner wealth, for we know that it constitutes "the kingdom of heaven," and makes us truly "rich toward God."

If a man had a large income, but was in the habit of depositing his money in a safe to which thieves had ready access, and to which they were in the habit of paying frequent visits, so that, when the man went to the safe to get his money, he could never be certain that there was any there, no matter how much he had deposited, such a man would scarcely be regarded wealthy, nor could his credit among business men be very good. In order to be counted wealthy and reliable in this world's estimation, a man must have, not only the ability to gain riches, but to safely care for them, and maintain a firm and constant control of them. Likewise, a man is not rich in the treasures of the kingdom of heaven, unless he has demonstrated the ability to maintain a firm and constant hold upon his spiritual riches, no matter what thieves and robbers, in the line of outward temptations, may do to take them away. Mere good impulses, and good intentions now and then, no matter how frequent or varied, do not make a man rich toward God. It is the retention and utilization of spiritual treasures, despite dangers, difficulties and temptations, that demonstrate how much treasure one has really laid up in heaven.

If a person is once thoroughly awakened to the fundamental importance of spiritual riches, so that he has had the experience, for a time, of keeping them safe and available in his consciousness, he soon learns that, for his own happiness, he cannot afford to let peace, joy and love escape him, whatever the temptation to distraction of thought. Nevertheless, at this stage of his development, he has only just begun to "enter into life." He has only learned to appreciate peace, joy and love in a negative way; he has only discovered that he cannot get on very well without them. He does not take much conscious notice of them when he has them; but only begins to think about them when he perceives that there is danger that he may lose them. There is yet more for him to learn, which is of vast importance.

There comes a time in the aspiring man's development when he begins to set a *positive* value upon desirable states of consciousness, when he begins to cultivate love in his consciousness, to watch its increase, and to experience joy in the accumulation, even more than the successful worldling enjoys the enlargement of his material possessions. He begins to discover new methods of increasing and using his store of love. He finds, for instance, that in doing a kindly and considerate deed for another, his own possession of peace, joy, love, and other mental riches, is increased; and, with his awakened sense, he becomes considerate for this increase far more than for a return in kind at the hands of the one to whom he had done a kindness, far more than for any material good he might receive. He has reached a point in his development where, in doing good deeds, he can realize that "his reward is with him," because the very doing of the good deed automatically brings him an increase of the wealth which he has learned to value more than all other goods. He has come to understand and appreciate Jesus' words when he said: "Do good, and lend, hoping for nothing again; and your reward shall be great, and ye shall be called the children of the Highest."

If one who had no musical education, were to attend a series of symphony concerts, they might not mean much to him at the start. They would bring him little satisfaction, even if they did not prove tiresome. But, as he continued to attend, he would gradually begin to appreciate the music, until after a time, he would find himself experiencing a positive and lively sense of pleasure and benefit. This change in his experience would not be because there had been any essential change in the character of the concerts, but it would come solely as the result of growth in his power of appreciation — of being able to set a value, in terms of consciousness, upon the music. Likewise, a person may reach a stage of development where much of peace and love and righteousness are within the range of his experience, and still get little positive joy from them; but if he begins to turn his attention to them, and to the experiences which increase his store of them, then he begins more and more to appreciate them; and as this comes to pass, his store of mental riches is ever increasing. Then, instead of being merely negatively peaceful and happy, it comes to pass that he finds, in the course of his experience, continual occasions for positive exhilaration and joy; and, although he knows that joy is the birthright of the children of God, he no longer takes these experiences of consciousness as "matters of course," but lives in wonderland, and constantly marvels at the goodness of God, who has conferred upon him the ability to possess, appreciate and enjoy such riches.

This thought, that we should become distinctly conscious of our mental states, and that we should watch the growth of our mental treasures, runs contrary to much that has been written. There are many who hold that as soon as a person begins to take account of his mental conditions, as soon as he begins to reckon his growth in love and in other spiritual virtues, he becomes self-conscious in an undesirable sense. But to consciously grow in the exercise and possession of divine love is not to become self-conscious, but God-conscious, since to dwell in love and appreciate love, the reflection of God, is to consciously dwell in God and appreciate Him, which is the prime duty of man. "Lay not up for yourselves treasures on earth, where moth and rust doth corrupt, and where thieves break through and steal, but lay up for yourselves treasures in heaven [in harmonious consciousness], where moth and rust do not corrupt and where thieves do not break through and steal; for where your treasure is, there will your heart be also."

It is true that a person might analyze his mental states, and take account of his growth in certain virtues, in such a way as to become self-righteous; but this is in no sense a necessary outcome of our learning to appreciate spiritual treasures, and to purposely take means of enlarging our possession of them and our joy in them.

Getting Rich

Once started along this road, there is infinite opportunity of growth and enlargement for every individual. The experiences of peace, joy, liberty and love, to which we all may and shall attain, cannot be measured, for they are infinite.

Before the individual has made any great degree of progress in "getting rich" along these lines, he begins to discover, more and more, that, except in a very secondary sense, neither the possession of material goods, nor the right use of them, is the source of desirable states of consciousness. We can gain a large experience of these mental treasures, and a firm hold upon them, only in proportion as we acquaint ourselves with God, and derive them directly from Him. We learn that He is the only source of unmixed good, and that even the good which we seem to get from and through matter is from Him, though much adulterated or distorted by the material medium. We experience good in connection with materiality, not because of it, but in spite of it. Love, joy, and peace are not properties of matter, and they are not found in material pursuits. They are everlasting manifestations of God, which are ever at hand. They may be gained and possessed without limit by any individual who becomes awake to their presence, and who is willing to work for them faithfully, intelligently and in right ways.

The worker along these lines also soon discovers that, while consciously seeking these mental treasures, and centering his attention primarily upon gaining them, such outward or material goods as he needs for harmonious living, while he is still forced to dwell in part in material sense, come his way without a large amount of conscious effort on his part. He finds the words of Christ to be literally true, "Seek ye first the kingdom of God and His righteousness, and all these things shall be added unto you." It is true, that in our present stage of experience, we cannot have large conscious possession of peace, joy and love without experiencing an increase of health and strength of body, as well as of material goods; and it is true, that if we strive most of all to make ourselves "rich toward God," we shall soon find ourselves not lacking either in strength, health, or worldly possessions according to our needs.

* * * * * * *

    A balanced man is one who can center his thought at will, be it in the solitude of the mountain vastness, or facing peril in the jungle; in the hurly-burly of affairs, or in the quiet of his favorite den. This is the realization of God — ever-present. It is the secret of all true achievement. A really poised man is a miracle, humanly speaking; it is he who has found the secret source of all power, solved his problem, and entered upon the life that is boundless and eternal.

H. F. Porter.

DIVINE LOVE MEETS ALL NEEDS

"Divine Love always has met and always will meet every human need." The literal truth of this sentence from *Science and Health*, by Mrs. Eddy, has been questioned by many. They have said, "Countless thousands of men have suffered and died from lack of good, drink, raiment, shelter, health and strength. Then how can it be said that divine Love has met their need?"

In the first place, it is readily perceived, on statement, that to meet a need is not to relieve the need, unless the supply provided is appropriated by the person who is in need. As we shall see presently, God does meet us with the supply for our every need, and that supply is always at hand, and always has been at hand for mankind in all ages; but God has provided that we must consciously appropriate this supply, and by the method which He has ordained. The need of every man has always been *met* with that which he needed; and if his necessity was not relieved, it was because he did not understand, or neglected to practice, the prescribed method of appropriation.

In absolute and final reality, and in present reality, food, drink, raiment, shelter, health, strength and life are purely spiritual, as the Scripture clearly states. "Man shall not live by bread alone, but by every word that proceedeth out of the mouth of God." "Except ye eat the flesh of the Son of man, and drink his blood, ye have no life in you." "Because thou sayest, I am rich, and increased with goods, and have need of nothing; and knowest not that thou art wretched, and miserable, and poor, and blind, and naked; I counsel thee to buy of me gold tried in the fire, that thou mayest be rich; and white raiment, that thou mayest be clothed, and that the shame of thy nakedness do not appear." "I will dwell in the house of the

Lord forever." "I shall yet praise him, who is the health of my countenance, and my God." "This is life eternal, that they might know thee, the only true God, and Jesus Christ whom thou hast sent."

Perceiving that the real and true supply for our needs is spiritual, we can at once understand that God all the time meets every man's need with His Spirit, which is substance, strength, harmony, life, and an everlasting dwelling place. "In Him, we live and move and have our being." Whoever appropriates this spiritual supply gains the kingdom of heaven.

But what about men's need for material food, drink, and raiment? Are not these human needs? Has God always met these needs? Yes, He has always *met* even these needs, although He has not forced the appropriation of the supply upon those who would not seek to gain it in the proper manner. These needs are not real, but only apparent; still, they are very imperative from humanity's present standpoint; and Christ Jesus has pointed out in clear and unmistakable language the right method of appropriating the supply. "Be not anxious, saying, What shall we eat? or, What shall we drink? or, Wherewithal shall we be clothed? For your heavenly Father knoweth that ye have need of all these things. But seek ye first the kingdom of God, and His righteousness; and all these things shall be added unto you." In other words, whoever sufficiently appropriates the real, spiritual food, drink, raiment, shelter, strength, health, and life, will infallibly have a sufficient supply of the material counterparts of these spiritual realities "added unto" him, as long as he has need of any material supply.

The greatest human need, even here and now, is more Spirit, rather than more matter. The trouble with most men is that, relatively, they have too much matter in proportion to their present vital possession of Spirit. If any man lacks material supply, it is a sure sign that he has not sufficient hold on Spirit, though the converse proposition is not true, that an abundant material supply is necessarily a sign that the owner is "rich toward God." But if any man lacks material supply, his first effort should be, not to gain more matter, but more of Spirit. If he does so, his need will not only be *met*, as it always was and always will be, far more than half way, but his need will be filled. "Blessed are they which hunger and thirst after righteousness [right-wise-ness]; for they shall be filled," not only with the kingdom of God, but even with the supply of their material needs.

So it is true that, "divine Love always has met and always will meet every human need"; and men will always find their need, not only *met*, but abundantly satisfied, if they will "seek first the kingdom of God and his righteousness."

* * * * * * *

Does God Know Evil?

"The Lord knoweth the way of the righteous; but the way of the ungodly shall perish." The way of the righteous is real and eternal, because God knows it. By inference and contrast the way of the ungodly shall perish because God does not know it. If God did know it, it would not perish, since anything in divine Mind cannot be lost therefrom, and so whatever is known to God, exists eternally. "God is light, and in Him is no darkness at all." That is, infinite Mind is all good, and there is in it no thought or knowledge of evil at all. God is "of purer eyes than to behold evil, and cannot look on iniquity."

THE LAW OF RIGHT FEELING

They should seek the Lord, if haply they might feel after him, and find him.
                                                            Paul

Science declares that Mind, not matter, sees, hears, feels, speaks.
                                                Mary Baker Eddy

The writer has observed that many students of Christian Science pay less attention to the government of the mental *feelings* than to the government of the *thoughts*. Yet the satisfaction of daily living is more directly a matter of the feelings than of the thoughts, and conditions of health are almost wholly determined for good or ill by the right or wrong activity of the feelings, though, of course, right understanding is necessary to right feeling. Many mistaken mental processes which are merely intellectual do not, on our present plane of experience, adversely affect the feelings, and so do not occasion suffering, either mental or physical; but wrong emotional processes constitute mental suffering or unhappiness, and, if persisted in, beget what is called physical disease. Right activity of the feelings, activity in accord with the nature of God, constitutes, in large measure, the riches of the kingdom of heaven, which are the only true riches.

Since God is the creator and governor of the universe, and is all-powerful and omnipresent, the various manifestations of God constitute the law of the universe, the law of being, the *law of every man's mentality*. Part of the changeless manifestations of God consist in love, joy, peace, and confidence in good; hence, these manifestations constitute the *law governing the feelings*, and any manifestation of human feeling at variance with these divine manifestations is false emotional activity. Fear, anxiety, worry, grief, doubt, anger, jealousy, envy, revenge, all are forms of false emotion.

On reflection, it is easy to perceive that there is absolutely no connection between opposites — no connection between falsehood and truth, or between evil and good. Consequently, there is absolutely no connection between love, joy, peace and confidence in good on the one hand, and fear, grief, anger, or doubt, or anything that can seem to occasion them on the other. For instance, the loss of a pocketbook containing money does not occur in the changeless realm of God, or Truth; it only occurs in the false, phenomenal realm of error. Hence, there is absolutely no legitimate connection between such a loss and joy and peace as states of mind. Joy and peace are not properties, or manifestations, of a full pocketbook; hence, they cannot possibly proceed from such a pocketbook. They are properties, or manifestations, of Spirit, God, and proceed from Him alone. The argument that there is a connection between a pocketbook and the joy and peace of the mind, is one of the deceptions of false sense, Satan.

The loss of a pocketbook would not tempt one to break the law of numbers in his thinking; it would not tempt one, for instance, to think that five times six are twenty-six. There is no connection between the loss of a pocketbook and one's thought about five times six; and as one attains to the Mind that was in Christ Jesus, there can be no more connection between the loss of a pocketbook and the state of his feelings than there is between such loss and his thought about five times six. Man's feelings can act only in accord with their source and Principle, God, and they are not affected by that which is not their source or Principle of being.

Yellowness, hardness, and opacity, are changeless manifestations of gold. Wherever gold is, there yellowness, hardness, and opacity are always found. The loss of a pocketbook could not in the slightest degree change the color of gold, or cause yellowness to depart from gold — either gold in the pocketbook or anywhere else in the world — since they depend solely on the nature of God; neither can such loss cause joy and peace to depart in the slightest degree from the mentality of a human being, if that mentality is stayed on God, and so is governed by the only law or truth of being.

Likewise, unfair or insulting human conduct has absolutely no relation to the love, joy, and peace which St. Paul speaks of as "fruits of the Spirit." These have neither their source nor their Principle in unjust or discordant human conduct; their source and Principle is God, and human mentality must learn to consent to the government of its feelings by God alone, and not by human behavior — otherwise, its government and its action are both false and afflictive.

All the misery of the human race is attributable to the fact that the human mind allows ignorance and false sense to enforce their claim that a connection exists between true feelings and material circumstance and human behavior, whereas no such connection exists. The only legitimate connection of feeling is with God. This is the truth, a part of that truth which Christ Jesus declared would make those who know it free from the ills of life.

If we but learn to say to ourselves, many times per day perchance, as occasion arises, "No connection (applying the phrase as a reminder that there is no necessary or reasonable relation) exists between seeming material loss, or unjust or unkind behavior on the part of human beings, and the love, joy, and peace which belong to us as children of God," then we will be protecting ourselves from the loss of the only riches which are real; we will live more happily, healthfully and prosperously even in a world sense, and more fully obey the command: "Lay not up for yourselves treasures on earth, where moth and rust corrupt, and where thieves break through and steal; but lay up for yourselves treasures in heaven [in daily spiritualized consciousness] where moth and rust do not corrupt, and where thieves do not break through and steal." Doing this, we shall "seek first the kingdom of God and His righteousness," and what we need to eat, drink and wear will infallibly be added unto us, notwithstanding any temporary seeming to the contrary. This is the promise of Christ, whose word cannot fail.

In fact, there is no legitimate connection between the activity of love, joy, peace and confidence in good, and weakness or pain of the body; but this is sometimes a little more difficult to demonstrate. What is called disease of the body is usually the result of one having entertained some false feeling masquerading as a mental state; and, if what may be termed the mental discord is first eliminated, the bodily ill will usually soon vanish. On the basis of the understanding and practice of the truth above set forth, it ought to be possible quickly to eliminate from consciousness lust, fear, worry, anxiety, grief, doubt, anger, jealously, envy, revenge, and the like. These are purely mental discords. In some cases, it may not be humanly possible to have a very full sense of joy and peace while suffering from weakness or pain; but if the mental discords above mentioned are thoroughly eliminated, the sense of weakness and pain will soon disappear. Then there will be nothing to interfere with a full realization of love, joy, peace and confidence in good.

Suppose that a boy, who was just commencing to study arithmetic, had an enemy, older than himself, who pretended to be his friend, and whom he believed to be his friend. If this pseudo-friend could persuade the boy that he ought to begin his study of arithmetic with fractions, and that, if he did so, he would, in this way, most readily learn addition, subtraction, multiplication, and division, he could prevent the boy from gaining a knowledge of arithmetic at all, or, at least, make it extremely difficult for him to do so. Likewise, if Satan, mortal belief, can persuade us that we should seek happiness, or harmonious consciousness, by commencing with the attainment of material prosperity, agreeable social recognition and bodily health, and that, if we do so, we shall, in this way, most readily attain joy, peace, and a loving attitude of mind, he will prevent us from attaining harmonious consciousness altogether, or at least make it exceedingly difficult for us to do so. In this way, we should be as badly misled as the boy would be, if he were persuaded to commence the study of arithmetic with fractions.

As before intimated, pain, weakness, and poverty are as unlike God, and so as untrue and unreal, as are fear, doubt, worry, grief, lust, jealousy, anger, and the like. But the writer has discovered from experience, that if he starts a patient working against pain, weakness, or poverty, both the patient's effort and his own work in behalf of the patient often fail of quick results, as is often true in the experience of all practitioners; and, as a consequence, the patient gets discouraged. But, when the patient is shown how to begin work for himself by combating purely mental discords, in the manner already indicated in this article, he finds himself winning victories from the start, and he is greatly encouraged, and is much more responsive to the practitioner's work. There is great wisdom in giving a beginner something to do that he can be sure to accomplish if he is diligent, rather than to set him a task at which, as a beginner, he is quite likely to fail. Since the writer definitely began to use this method of procedure, he has healed quite a large number of patients who have had treatment for considerable time by various practitioners, and have been studying and working for themselves, and all without much success. The healing was accomplished by starting them to work at demonstrating right feeling, rather than at demonstrating health or outward harmony. They had failed for so long because they had never started right. Beginning at the right point in their work, the health and outward harmony were soon attained.

In the Father-Mother God, Truth or intelligence is the divine Father, and Love is the divine Mother. "White-robed purity will unite in one person masculine wisdom and feminine love." (*Science and Health*) As the child in the early stages of its human life has, and needs to have, much more to do with its mother than with its father, so the "babe in Christ," the beginner in Christian Science, has need to work even more in Love, through demonstrating right

The Law of Right Feeling

feeling, than in Truth, through demonstrating right thinking; though as he attains spiritual manhood, he must come into the full recognition and demonstration of both Truth and Love.

Let one of our watchwords be, "No connection" between the good of the mind and discordant human or material circumstances. We can always say to ourselves that God is a sufficient reason for not fearing, not doubting, not worrying, not grieving.

At our present stage of development, we cannot wholly, or even largely, withdraw our *thoughts* from the consideration of discords and difficulties, but, here and now, we can learn to keep our *feelings* with God, harmony, *all the time*. The oft quoted motto, "Let nothing disturb the harmony of your thoughts," might be revised to our profit, so that it shall read, "Let nothing disturb the harmony of your feelings."

Having mediatorial intelligence, we can not only know and declare Truth, but can also consider and uncover error and reverse it in favor of the truth. Having divine love with which to dissolve error, we are perfectly equipped for the service of God on the human plane, and for the true service of ourselves. But if we allow the feelings to be engaged with and ruled by discord, we can serve nothing but Satan.

We should not allow our *feelings* to be governed by the evidence before the senses however much our *thought* must rest upon outward circumstances while engaged in overcoming human discords and difficulties.

* * * * * * *

Jesus' life, outwardly, was one of the most troubled lives that was ever lived. Tempest and tumult, tumult and tempest — the waves breaking over it all the time. But the inner life was a sea of glass. The great calm was always there. At any moment you might have gone to Him and found rest.

Henry Drummond.

THE CONSCIOUSNESS THAT HEALS
(From the *Christian Science Sentinel*, Sept. 12, 1908)

In Christian Science, great emphasis is laid upon the Scriptural statements that God is Spirit; God is eternal; God is perfect, and God is the only cause and creator. The creations of God would naturally and inevitably bear His characteristics, and not characteristics opposite to Him. Therefore, the real universe and man were created like to God — spiritual, eternal, and perfect — and they so remain, because God's all-power preserves them as He made them. And God, Spirit, knows or discerns His universe and His children as they are — that is, spiritual, eternal, and perfect. If we could discern the universe in the same way that Spirit discerns it, then that would be spiritual discernment on our part; but we are not able to exercise spiritual discernment through the physical senses, nor ever shall we, "for the carnal mind is enmity against God." We may, however, exercise spiritual discernment in spite of the physical senses by reasoning from God as premise, thus determining what the character of man and the universe must be, and obeying the Scriptural rule of "comparing spiritual things with spiritual."

If we have spiritual discernment, we have faith; for the two are identical. And if we know, or discern, the universe and man as God knows them, then in our thinking, or consciousness, we reflect the divine thinking, just as Jesus did. When we do this, we know the power of Mind as did the Master; and the Mind, or consciousness, which Jesus had, was that consciousness which healed the sick, raised the dead, and cast out devils (evils). Having freely received this consciousness from God, he freely gave it to as many as would receive it; and it is our duty to reflect this same consciousness. St. Paul exhorts, "Let this mind be in you, which was also in Christ Jesus."

The Consciousness that Heals

To have and to exercise this healing consciousness, and obtain results therefrom, several things are requisite. First of all, we must understand that all God's ideas and their expression are spiritual, eternal, and perfect; but it is far from sufficient to accept this intellectually, as a creed to be recited in church and on other formal occasions. On the other hand, this view of all that is, must become a part of our habitual thinking. The tendency with us, as mortals, is to let our thoughts, moment by moment, dwell upon the subjects presented by the physical senses, and to be thus directed by what seems to transpire in our bodies and in the so-called physical world. In other words, it is considered "natural" for us to let our thoughts drift with the current of sense testimony. The duty set before us is to make head against this current and never to drift with it a moment, when we can avoid it.

Our problem is to gain gradually, and as rapidly as possible, the ability to keep habitually our thoughts on the plane of spiritual discernment. This we shall accomplish by purposely lifting our thoughts, moment by moment, away from the presentations of the bodily senses, and by fixing them on God and on the nature of His spiritual creation. If sense testimony obtrudes itself on us so much that we cannot ignore it, we may then deny and reverse it in favor of the spiritual truth, until its claims are so much silenced that they retire into the background. If we persistently take control of and direct our thoughts, in a few weeks or months the spiritual attitude of mind will become habitual, and most of the time there will abide in consciousness a realization of the perfection of man and all real things; that all are expressions of the spiritual, eternal, and perfect — and this quite independently of the fact that at the given time we may be "treating" ourselves or another for sickness, sin, or any other trouble. To have such a consciousness is to "pray without ceasing."

This consciousness must be not merely intellectual; it must be transfused with love — the love of God and the love of His whole creation, as being spiritual and good, and therefore lovable.

By conscious, persistent effort, we can acquire the habit of having our thoughts and feelings turn to God, and to the right perception and active knowing and loving of His creation; and the time soon comes when this no longer calls for effort, for our thoughts and feelings run naturally in such channels.

Finally, the spiritual consciousness, to the degree that it is attained, must find expression in our lives, so far as it is possible to make the demonstration. If loyal to the spiritual program of life, we shall not seek material things as an end in themselves, or under the belief that they are real; but we shall know that substance is Spirit and matter is only shadow. Then we will seek "first the kingdom of God, and his righteousness," and let the material take a secondary place, until such time as the appearance of it is destroyed by the fuller realization of Truth. We shall not recognize intelligence or power in matter by taking drugs; and we shall not, when we can harmoniously avoid it, seek the pleasures of the flesh.

Such a spiritual consciousness exemplified in daily life will be, to a large degree, Godlike, and will be transparent to the divine Mind, even as a pane of glass is transparent to sunlight. Mrs. Eddy says, "The manifestation of God through mortals is as light passing through the windowpane." (*Science and Health*) In like manner, the light of Truth passes through a spiritualized consciousness, and destroys all belief in sin and disease, and ultimately destroys the belief in death and matter. Such a consciousness is a window open toward heaven. It lets in the light for ourselves; and whoever turns to us for help, may experience enough of the light of Truth and Love shining through to heal him of his diseases. To change the example, if we have such a consciousness, it is as a mirror reflecting the divine Mind; and by consciously directly our spiritual thoughts, we may reflect the healing rays of Truth and Love upon whom we will.

From this description, it will be seen that in Christian Science it is the divine Mind and the reflected consciousness thereof which heals the sick. It will also be seen how radically different is this process from faith-cure, based on blind belief, and from processes of hypnotism or suggestive therapeutics, wherein a human consciousness which accepts matter, sin, and disease as real is the supposed curative agent. It must be very evident that Christian Science healing is based on the divine Mind, God, while all other forms of mental treatment are based more or less on the human, carnal mind, which, as Paul says, "is enmity against God."

The state of consciousness above described exemplifies this verse from Psalms: "Blessed is the man that walketh not in the counsel of the ungodly, nor standeth in the way of sinners, nor sitteth in the seat of the scornful. But his delight is in the law of the Lord; and in his law doth he meditate day and night. And he shall be like a tree planted by the rivers of water, . . . his leaf also shall not wither; and whatsoever he doeth shall prosper."

* * * * * * *

Some people speak of being repellent to others, or of being repelled by others. It is only a sense of self that is repelled. Imagine light being repelled by darkness! Imagine any sinner, however great his sin, repelling the all-powerful, the all-embracing love of Christ, manifested through Jesus! Is there any case on record of Jesus being repelled? Did he come to turn away from sinners, or to save sinners from their sins? Let us become so unselfed that there is nothing in us to be repelled. Then, too, we shall not repel others.

PRAYER

To make this subject plain, let us first consider the steps by which a young man prays his way through college.

1. *Recognition.* Any young man who, of his own volition, registers in a college for a course, with an intelligent sense of what he is doing, recognizes that the college administers to its students a body of knowledge, and that this knowledge is in existence, ready to be administered, before the student goes there. The young man does not expect any knowledge, any facts or laws, to be created for his special benefit. Moreover, if he stops to think, he recognizes that neither this college, nor any other, nor all of them combined, have any monopoly of the facts and laws which they teach. All these facts and laws are just as much present in any man's home as they are in any college, and a knowledge of them could be gained in any man's home. The college is simply a more convenient place in which to gain this knowledge, because the college arranges the knowledge in the right order of presentation, and parcels it out in daily portions of the proper amount for the student to master, and gives him guidance and discipline, which he could not get at home — at least not without a very competent tutor. He could do the work at home, though not so easily.

2. *Desire.* Having recognized that the college has a body of knowledge to administer, the student, to succeed, must desire that knowledge. If he goes to college with the right purpose, he does not go for the buildings, nor for the faculty, nor for the amusements, but with a great desire for a knowledge of the facts and laws which he has recognized to be already in existence.

3. *Appropriation through concentration and drill.* Recognition and desire are fundamental to the young man's gaining the body of knowledge which the college administers, but they are not

sufficient. To succeed, the student must, each day, concentrate his consciousness upon the daily portion of the facts and laws allotted to him in the various branches which he is studying. Nor is it sufficient for him to study each fact and law until he clearly sees that it is true. He may have to spend considerable labor to do even this, but he must do more. He must go over and over these facts and laws, and drill them into his memory, into his consciousness, else he will not have command of them, either at examination time, or in his succeeding lessons, or when he needs them to do practical work.

The average college student drills the facts and laws in any subject into his mind sufficiently to enable him to have command of them until he has passed the examinations on that subject, and on related subjects; but how few of the facts and laws, taught in a college course, does the average student drill into his consciousness so thoroughly that he has a life-long command of them, so that he can make instant use of them at any time when it would suit his convenience or pleasure to do so? Only of the facts and laws of which he has gained an ineradicable and read-on-demand knowledge, can he be said to have gained an absolute mastery.

During the process of concentration and drill, the student has obstacles to contend with. In the first place, he has to overcome the inertia of ignorance, the difficulty of seeing and understanding the subject matter which he is studying. But, with many, an even greater difficulty is to rule out distracting thoughts, and keep the consciousness fixed with continuity, hours at a time, upon the subjects being studied. The young man who cannot, during his study hours, keep thoughts of the dance he went to the night before, or of the theatre party he is going to on Saturday night, or of the next week's football match, out of his mind for the most part, will not make much of a success in college. The difficulty of doing this is often very great, but most students do it, in spite of the difficulty. Distracting thoughts incident to disease of more or less severity, homesickness, anxiety over money matters, and many others, also have to be sternly ruled out of the mind, in order to study successfully; and many accomplish this task.

4. *Application.* Nothing so fixes facts and laws, learned in theory, in the consciousness, in such a way as to give a mastery of them, as an application of them, as fast as learned, to practical conditions; and the best college attend to it, that their students shall be induced to make practical application of their theoretical knowledge to the largest possible extent. This not only helps them while in college, but fits them for work in the world.

The student who properly attends to the elements of recognition, desire, appropriation, and application, in connection with the body of knowledge which the college is administering, will, without the slightest doubt, graduate from the college in due time and with high honors. If he properly attends to these four elements, he has daily maintained an attitude of prayer, when prayer is rightly understood, for true prayer always includes the elements above mentioned. It includes desire, but it never includes an expectation of, or an asking for, any change in the objects of desire, or in that which is addressed in prayer. It recognizes that all the change must take place in the one who is praying, lifting him from ignorance to knowledge, from bondage to freedom, and from evil to good.

Now let us consider how it works out on a higher and more important field of endeavor.

What practically all well-meaning people in the world are striving for is the attainment of holiness, health and plenty — in other words, harmony. Religious people recognize that the source of these is God, and that it is a duty as well as a privilege to make these things a subject of prayer. What is the proper process? It is important to know, lest we should "ask and have not, because we ask amiss."

1. *Recognition.* Holiness, health (harmony, strength), and plenty, are laws of God; they are the eternal manifestations of His being. Since God is omnipresent, these manifestations are omnipresent; and since He is infinite, these manifestations are infinite and inexhaustible, and are ever at hand. So we should never expect God, or ask Him, to create any holiness, health, or supply for

us, or in any way to change Himself or His laws. If we do so, we shall "ask amiss." But we should recognize that God has already provided for us all good, and has placed it nearer to us than the air we breathe, as near to every man as are the facts of the multiplication table, which are at hand, ready to be learned and appropriated where a man is. This is what Jesus meant, when he said: "And therefore I say unto you, Have faith that whatever you ask for in prayer is already granted you, and you will find that it will be." (*Twentieth Century New Testament*)

2. *Desire.* Without desire for holiness, health and plenty, and without desiring them from their only true source, God, we shall have no more success in attaining them than would a college student, who, though attending college, had no real desire for the knowledge there administered. To *say* that we desire, is not sufficient. *The desire must be real.* Said Jesus, "Blessed are they which do *hunger and thirst* after righteousness; for they shall be filled." In *Science and Health*, Mrs. Eddy writes: "The danger from [audible] prayer is that it may lead us into temptation. By it we may become involuntary hypocrites, uttering desires which are not real and consoling ourselves in the midst of sin with the recollection that we have prayed over it or mean to ask forgiveness at some later day."

3. *Appropriation through concentration and drill.* We are born as ignorant of true holiness, health, and supply, and of their source, as we are of arithmetic, language, or chemistry; and we shall never gain a mastery of the harmony of life in its various phases with any less effort, or in any different manner, than we gain a mastery of the forms of worldly knowledge taught in school and college. If we wish to gain real possession of holiness, health, and plenty, we must concentrate our thought upon them, and upon their relation to God, until we understand what they really are. But theoretical understanding is far from being sufficient. Having seen and understood what these forms of harmony are, they belong to us in the same sense that the facts of the multiplication table belong to

us if we are willing to put forth the requisite effort to gain them. It next behooves us to hold our thought to the fact that harmony is the law of God, and is really the law of our being. We must hold it there consecutively by the hour, rigorously excluding all other thoughts, just as the child holds his thought to the multiplication table, with repetition after repetition, and application upon application, in order to absorb it indelibly into his consciousness.

During this process of concentration and drill, our greatest obstacles are intruding thoughts, trying to distract our attention — temptations of sinful desire; thoughts of pleasure, innocent enough in themselves, but out of place during our period of prayer; feelings of fear, anxiety, worry; feelings of pain or weakness; thoughts along a score of lines opposite to the law of harmony which we are trying to master. In order for rapid growth, all such distracting thoughts must be sternly ruled out of our consciousness for a considerable consecutive period of each day, and as much as possible during all the day. Our thoughts and feelings must be consciously fastened upon harmony in its various manifestations, until we have permanently absorbed it into our consciousness or identified our consciousness with it.

In this connection, we may recall such Biblical counsel as follows: "Work out your own salvation with watchful care. Remember, it is God, who, in his kindness, is at work within you, enabling you both to will and to work." (*Twentieth Century New Testament*) "What I say unto you I say unto all, Watch." "Pray without ceasing." "Let us not be weary in well-doing; for in due season, we shall reap if we faint not." "For precept must be upon precept, precept upon precept; line upon line, line upon line." And from *Science and Health*, Mrs. Eddy writes, "Stand porter at the door of thought. Admitting only such conclusions as you wish realized in bodily results, you will control yourself harmoniously. When the condition is present which you say induces disease, whether it be air, exercise, heredity, contagion, or accident, then perform your office as porter and shut out these unhealthy thoughts and fears.

Exclude from mortal mind the offending errors. The issues of pain or pleasure must come through mind, and like a watchman forsaking his post, we admit the intruding belief, forgetting that through divine help we can forbid this entrance." "Hold thought steadfastly to the enduring, the good, and the true, and you will bring these into your experience proportionably to their occupancy of your thoughts."

4. *Application.* Nothing so quickly and so thoroughly gives us mastery of the law of harmony, after we theoretically understand what it is, as its constant application to the problems of daily living. As above indicated, until we have thoroughly accomplished our tasks, we should set aside some portion of each day for concentrated and consecutive direction of our thought to and upon the law of harmony, even as the college student has his periods of consecutive study; but, in addition to this, we should make use of our knowledge — that harmony really is the law and the power of being — to cast out of our consciousness feelings of fear, worry, doubt, sin, and pain at the very moment that these intruders try to gain entrance. If any of these forms of error seem to have gained permanent lodgment in our consciousness, as in the case of chronic sin or disease, we may well contend with these more especially during our periods of consecutive work or prayer; but throughout the day, we should apply our knowledge of harmony to the prompt ejection of any feelings of discord along new or unusual lines, which we detect springing up in our minds. This will be a most valuable application of what we are learning and striving for.

Most people have really acquired a mastery of the fundamentals of arithmetic. They could stand an examination at any time, at a moment's notice. If any ordinary problem presents itself in their business, they have immediate command of the knowledge with which to solve it. They do not have to consult a book, or to refresh their memory. They have no fear that the requisite knowledge is not there. When they have reached this stage, they do not have to study these fundamentals of arithmetic any more, or make any conscious effort with regard to them. They have merely to use the knowledge when occasion presents itself. They have so assimilated this knowledge that they do not hunger or thirst for it any more, since it springs up in them an inexhaustible well of water, ready for instant use.

Whoever recognizes that harmony — holiness, health, plenty — is the fact of being, and is ever at hand, eternal, changeless, and inexhaustible, the perpetual manifestation of God; and whoever desires that harmony in all its manifestations with his whole heart; and whoever will concentrate his thought and feeling upon this law, and hold his mind to it, and drill it into his consciousness, and make continued application of it, with the persistence, watchfulness, and patience that the average person has spent upon the fundamentals of arithmetic, such a person may be sure of attaining the same mastery of holiness, health and plenty. Then he will have no fear of losing them. He will not have to strive so hard for them as he once did. He will merely have to use his demonstrable knowledge of them occasionally to rule out discord, just as the average person has to use his knowledge of arithmetic occasionally to solve a problem; but he will have no more fear that he will be unable to overcome discord than the average person entertains a fear that he cannot add a grocery bill on occasion.

A person who has acquired such a demonstrable and ready-on-demand knowledge of the harmony of God in its various manifestations, has fed upon the bread of life, and to him the following words of Jesus properly apply: "He that eateth of this bread shall live forever." "Whosoever drinketh of the water that I shall give him shall never thirst; but the water that I shall give him shall be in him a well of water springing up into everlasting life."

* * * * * * *

Matter

  Matter makes itself known to us by the testimony of the senses. We see it, hear it, smell it, taste it, touch it. But observe, that, after all, this is indirect testimony. These impressions are all of them simply brain impressions. We see, hear, smell, taste, touch, in our consciousness only. We cannot assert therefore that matter exists apart from this consciousness. Science has nothing to say about the ultimate nature of matter. Science studies matter simply as a fact of human experience. We are not concerned in physics with what things really are, but solely with their properties and behavior. Physics neither offers nor seeks an explanation of the universe. It leaves all such problems to metaphysics.
From the Textbook on Physics by Henderson and Woodhull, of Columbia University.

FROM SICKNESS TO HEALTH

Matter is non-intelligent, even if it were real, which it is not. Matter, so-called, possesses neither consciousness nor the power of motion. It cannot plan its own states. It cannot rearrange itself, whether in the mass or in molecular relations. Matter, so-called, is a belief or shadow of substance, which mortal mind images forth as a medium in which and through which mortal mind can depict its operations. Therefore all states and conditions of matter, whether of the mortal body or other manifestations of matter, are determined by mortal mind, unless, through the operation of scientific Christianity, mortal mind has been brought under control by the conscious application of divine Mind — in which case the body is, in a sense, controlled by divine Mind, and continues to be, more and more, until such time as the belief of matter is completely dispelled.

It is well to understand what some phases of the mortal belief are, and certain claims of mortal mind are herewith set forth. If a person entertains in his consciousness, in an habitual way, anger, anxiety, grief, malice, covetousness, discontent, lust, envy, self-condemnation, or any inharmonious mental state or any mental state that is unlike the divine Mind, that mental condition is almost sure, sooner or later, to be pictured forth in some inharmonious or ungodlike condition of the body, named disease, whether organic or inorganic, so-called. Any of these inharmonious or ungodlike mental states, if habitual, gradually result in impeded and irregular action of one or more of the bodily organs, resulting in the development of poisons in the system, and in malnutrition and the imperfect assimilation of food. These conditions tend to increase, and almost any kind of a disease may result. Almost any up-to-date physician would agree that this is so.

From Sickness to Health

A gentleman of the author's acquaintance went into the office of an expert blood analyst, and had a drop of blood drawn from his wrist, he being at the time in an ordinary, contented frame of mind. Microscopic and other analysis of the drop showed the blood to be pure. Then the gentleman purposely thought about a matter concerning which it was easy for him to become angry. After twenty minutes of this, he had a drop of blood drawn, and the analysis showed the presence of both pus and bile. This fact ought to make it evident how disease often starts.

  The foregoing is a statement and illustration of the workings of mortal mind, error, and represents a condition of affairs to be overcome; and the mortal-mind cause, so-called, has to be overcome before the mortal-mind effect, so-called, can be overcome, another way of saying which is, that the sin must be overcome before the disease resulting from it can be overcome. The inharmonious and un-godlike mental conditions must be corrected, and harmonious and Godlike mental conditions must be established in their places, before the disease can be healed. Sometimes the realization of the practitioner, or of the patient himself when he is reading the Bible or Christian Science literature with the true understanding, may be so clear and absolute as to overcome both the sin and the disease in a few moments, or in a single treatment. In that case, the mortal-mind cause and mortal mind effect are both overcome as part of one and the same act. However, where the healing is not immediate, it is worth while to gain it by faithful and continued work. Under such a program, the chief effort of the patient and practitioner should be to overcome the inharmonious mental habits, being sure that, as soon as they are overcome, or very soon after, the disease will disappear. Some of the following suggestions will apply to one person and some to another. Each will doubtless be able to pick out what applies to himself or herself.

  Are you tempted to be frequently angry at your fellowmen, or at yourself, or at animals and things which are around you? "Cease from anger, and forsake wrath: fret not yourself in any wise to do evil." "Be not hasty in your spirit to be angry: for anger resteth in the bosom of fools." "He that hath no rule over his own spirit is like a city that is broken down." "Let all bitterness, and wrath, and anger, and clamour and evil speaking, be put away from you, with all malice."

Are you tempted to entertain and dwell upon lustful thoughts? Remember that the lusts of the flesh are not ordained of God, and are not known to God. They have no part in the divine Mind. They do not belong to the true man, which is your true selfhood, and which it is your business to demonstrate. "Be ye perfect, even as your Father in heaven is perfect." Entertain no thought or desire which your heavenly Father does not entertain. "Let no man say when he is tempted, I am tempted [tried] of God: for God cannot be tempted with evil, neither tempteth He any man: but every man is tempted when he is drawn away of his own lust and enticed. When lust hath conceived, it bringeth forth sin, and sin, when it is finished, bringeth forth [disease and] death. Do not err, my beloved brethren. Every good gift and every perfect gift is from above [and not from the earth or from the flesh] and cometh down from the Father of lights, with whom is no variableness, neither shadow of turning. Of His own will begat He us with the word of truth [not by any fleshly process], that we should be a kind of first fruit of His creatures. Wherefore, lay aside all filthiness and superfluity of naughtiness, and receive with meekness the engrafted word which is able to save your souls."

Are you tempted to continued grief over the loss of some cherished possession or over the so-called death of some loved one? Know that God has made all that really is, and that nothing which He has made can be destroyed. Know that no real good is, in truth, separated from you for an instant, and know that it is not in the power of error to keep you very long from realizing this fact. All that seems lost to you will soon be restored to you with a more perfect and satisfying possession or understanding thereof — and the sooner in proportion as you know this to be true, and have confidence in the imperishability of that which is good. Nothing is lost in truth, nor is the realization thereof lost very long to those who know this fact. "I would that you sorrow not as those who know not the gospel." God does not grieve over anything. He has no occasion to. In truth, you are His image and likeness; and you have no occasion for grief, if you do not allow yourself to be deceived by appearances, but, on the contrary, hang on to your scientific knowledge of things as they are. The world thinks that it is a virtue to grieve under certain conditions, and that it would be unnatural not to do so; but do not be deceived by the world's judgment. There is no virtue in grief. The Christian who really believes his faith, has little occasion for grief. Put it out of mind as not belonging to your high calling in Christ Jesus, if you would be holy, happy and well.

Are you tempted to be anxious about anything? Are you given to worry and fretting? No person ever bettered his condition in the least by entertaining any such sentiments; but many have done themselves, in appearance, incalculable harm by cherishing anxiety and worry. Do your duty by God, by your fellowmen, and by yourself, hour by hour, and day by day, as well as you know how, and let it rest at that. "Why are ye anxious for the morrow, what ye shall eat, or what ye shall drink, or wherewithal ye shall be clothed? Seek ye first the kingdom of God, and His righteousness, and all these things shall be added unto you." Do the best thing you can discover at all times. Having done that, "be careful [full of care] for nothing." As someone once said: "If you can do anything about it, why don't you? And if you can't, what is the use of worrying about it?" But if you believe God, you have no occasion to worry. If you really believe and trust Him, your needs will be met, day by day, whether you can see the way in advance or not.

Are you doubtful or discouraged because you are not healed quicker? That is the devil's device to keep you in an inharmonious state of mind, so that, in belief, your food will not assimilate, your bodily organs will not act properly, and poisons will continue to be secreted in your system. Do not be caught by this snare of the devil. Know that God made man; that all God's works are perfect; that health and harmony are eternal laws of God, and are present facts. Resting in this assurance, be hopeful, cheerful, patient and persistent. Maintain the joy of the Lord. Rule out all inharmonious and ungodlike emotions and sentiments. Keep them out by relying on God and by meditating on His law. If you do this persistently, the mortal mind causes of your trouble will be removed; your food will assimilate better; malnutrition will gradually cease; poisons will cease to be formed; the poisons already in your system, in belief, will be gradually eliminated; new and healthy tissues will be built up. If often takes time to accomplish this, but what of it? You entertained wrong mental states for weeks and months before the resulting disease developed. Is it any wonder that you should be required to entertain right and God-like habits of thought for weeks before the disease disappears? And do you not see that if you allow yourself to vacillate between hope and fear, between confidence and doubt, between trust in God and anxiety, and do not trust God with your whole heart, you are delaying your healing just so much? It is practically certain that if you maintain a confident, hopeful, cheerful frame of mind, *without interruption*, for a number of weeks consecutively, beneficial physical results will be in evidence. "Why art thou cast down, O my soul? and why art thou disquieted within me? Hope thou in God; for I shall yet praise Him, who is the health of my countenance, and my God."

  The summation of the matter is: If you want to be well, believe in God, and the all-power and all-presence of good, and the essential nothingness and impermanency of evil in its every manifestation; cultivate and maintain God-like qualities of mind; cast out and refuse to entertain all ungodlike qualities of mind, however much excuse there may seem to be for entertaining them; keep your confidence in God, and keep on doing it; and, meanwhile, place your sole reliance for healing upon Spirit, and withdraw your reliance absolutely from matter, whether in the form of drugs, or in any other form, thus honoring the Lord your God with your whole trust and with your whole reliance. Follow this program faithfully and without cessation; and your reward is sure; and it will come in such time as is really for your best good. To carry out this program, do not hesitate at any amount of effort, nor at any reasonable expense, nor at any sacrifice of worldly plans and pleasures; for that which you will attain as the result of this program will be the salvation of your soul, the being made God-like in your consciousness.

Your particular disease may be one which was not caused in the beginning by any inharmonious mental state which you were cherishing, but may have been caused by an accident, by being poisoned in some way, by the mortal belief of contagion, by the mortal belief of having taken germs into your system through drinking water, or food, or otherwise, or by any one of a variety of so-called causes of disease extraneous to your thought. Even if this be the case, yet you probably have been through a long period of fear, anxiety, doubt, and discouragement incident to the disease and to complications in your affairs which your diseased condition may have resulted in. Hence, very likely, there has developed in your system, in belief, more or less of the inactive and poisonous conditions which result from fear, anxiety, and discouragement, and, in the bodily manifestation.

Hence, to heal the disease requires the overcoming and casting out of fear, anxiety, doubt, and discouragement, almost or quite as much as though the disease had been caused originally by some untoward mental condition. Little or nothing may stand in the way of your healing except the inharmonious and ungodlike mental conditions which you are cherishing, whether your disease originated in such conditions or not. If the disease did not originate in improper mental emotions which you were cherishing, then the disease came on without sin on your own part; and it ought to be easily overcome, if you have not allowed sin (ungodlike mental emotions) to creep in and occupy your consciousness because of the disease. As said before, you should "right about face," place your hope, your trust, your confidence, in God, and keep on doing so without vacillation. Then the disease will commence to yield, and be completely overcome, whatever its original cause may have been.

The whole universe is ruled absolutely by God, Love, unadulterated good. If you actually believe this, you have nothing to fear, nothing to be anxious about, nothing to be discouraged about. It is only the cherishing of fear, anxiety, doubt, and discouragement which can long cloud over from your realization the health, harmony, strength and abundance which God has provided from the foundation of the world, and which are already yours, and which are constantly closer to you than the air you breathe, and from which, in reality, you can never get away. Therefore, don't be afraid; don't be anxious; don't grieve; don't be discouraged: *you cannot afford to.* Hope and trust in God; and keep at it, through thick and thin of the clouds of mortal error, and they will soon vanish entirely.

* * * * * * *

All the good law and all the good order which the state or church enjoys today may be traced back over some route to the words and deeds of men who rebelled against the kind of law and the kind of order that they found administered by its 'constituted guardians'; to men who dared to appeal from the 'keepers of divine truth' to divine truth itself — from the 'trustees of God' to God himself.

WORKING IN TRUTH

"Trust in the Lord with all thy heart, and lean not to thine own understanding, but in all thy ways acknowledge Him, and He shall direct thy paths."

To trust in God is not an inactive state of mind, and is not most apropos when everything is, to human sense, smooth sailing. We have more need of trust in God in time of outward storm, than in time of outward calm.

To rightly trust in God is not a passive condition. It is to actively lay hold on and declare the supremacy, allness, and potency of the everlasting laws of God, good, and to keep doing this every moment, until we have won inward peace, and not only peace, but joy, and not only joy, but the conscious sense of power — the realization that no error can stand before us because we have consciously taken our stand with the law, the dynamic energy, of God. We are fighting with the sword of the Spirit, which is the Word of God.

We should keep ourselves in this active realization of peace, joy in good, and power, at least part of the time daily. If we can so reverse the arguments of mortal mind as to rise into this sense of spiritual power at those special times when error would argue the reality of discouragement, injustice, grief, separation, etc., to us, we shall maintain a peaceful consciousness all of the time. And we can rise at times into the active, assertive realization of the presence and power of unity, justice, and love, so that outward discord will soon disappear.

Error is most surely making headway in enforcing its so-called law, when it has induced us to listen to its argument for the reality of injustice, separation, misunderstanding, discouragement, grief, and other falsehoods; and this is just the time when error needs to be met. It is not wise to say to ourselves, Well, I will yield to this sense of discouragement, or smarting, or grief, or injustice, or what not, until the mood passes, and then, when I am not under temptation, when I feel calmer, I will work in the truth. To assume this attitude, is to allow error to entrench itself, which is always unwise and sometimes dangerous; it is to allow ourselves to get into a frame of mind where we are liable to do or say some unwise thing against our own right interests. Moreover, to assume this attitude is to sacrifice a golden opportunity.

If we make the initial effort, we shall find that we can rise to a clearness and strength of realization of the presence and power of good at the very time when temptation to doubt, discouragement, grief, anxiety, and the like is upon us, to a degree that we cannot attain to at any other time. The really brave man experiences a sense of courage in the face of danger that he could not possibly conjure up at a time when no danger was apparent. So the true Christian can realize a degree of love, at the very time when error is trying to argue hate or unfairness or jealousy, that he otherwise would find difficulty in attaining.

Likewise, the true Christian, if he takes advantage of his opportunity, can realize joy in good — joy in the knowledge that it is in his power to enforce good, joy in the certain prospect of seeing error, injustice, falsehood, narrowness, go down before the mental enforcement of Love — to a degree that, at his present stage of growth, he cannot attain to except when he is spurred to rise to such a spiritual height by a conscious reaction against outward suggestions or occasions for grief, anxiety, or fear. And so the true Christian meets every outward phase of error, in the very moment of its appearing, with a superlative realization of the presence and potency of the opposing phase of good, and of his power through right mental work to enforce that phase of good to the overcoming and total destruction of the manifest phase of error. Thus hatred, malice, envy, jealousy, revenge, are met with the realization and mental enforcement of Love; injustice with the realization of justice; fear with the realization and enforcement of the omnipotence of God, good.

Just as the courage of the trained soldier rises instantaneously and automatically in the face of danger, likewise we can rapidly so train ourselves that the disposition to the mental enforcement of the law of God, good, shall spring up in our consciousness instantaneously and spontaneously upon the appearance of error in any phase — and this, too, as previously remarked, to a degree that we could not now attain to except in the face of some obstacle to be overcome. And it is this instantaneous, superlative realization and enforcement of good that is of supreme value in overcoming and destroying error. It does not permit us to consent to the reality of error anywhere from a few hours to a few days before waking up to combat it, thus allowing error to entrench itself in our consciousness and in the outward situation; but it meets error on the spot, and with a clearness and potency of realization to which we could not attain if we were less prompt in turning to God. Thus error is stifled and cast into outer darkness, its native nothingness, often in the very moment of its seeming birth, and usually before it has assumed large apparent proportions.

In dealing with mental errors, such as anger, jealousy, injustice, selfishness, narrowness, as manifest through those with whom we are associated, it is usually wiser not to say very much audibly; or to be drawn into discussions, but to mentally enforce the law of God. "Though we walk in the flesh, we do not war after the flesh [by human speech and understanding]; for the weapons of our warfare are not carnal, but mighty through God [Love] to the pulling down of strongholds, casting down imaginations and every high thing that exalteth itself against the knowledge of God, and bringing into captivity every thought [within or without] to the obedience of Christ." If you are obeying God, and are thus the child of God, "no weapon that is formed against thee shall prosper; and every tongue that shall rise against thee in judgment thou shalt condemn. This is the heritage of the servants of the Lord, and their righteousness is of me saith the Lord." Let us mentally enforce this law. Let us train ourselves to do it immediately and automatically and confidently whenever error asserts itself. "Watch." "Pray [aspire after, realize and enforce good] without ceasing." "Be instant in season, out of season." Thus shall we uniformly have peace, joy and victory in God — and ofttimes more in the very moments when error is most assertive, until, at the last, we shall have part in the final victory when all error shall disappear, never to appear again.

Thus far the overcoming of discord in the mental realm has been spoken of; but discord in the so-called physical realm is to be removed in the same way. Apparent disease or weakness in the body should be instantly met with the realization and enforcement of the laws of harmony and strength, and the sense of poverty or accident should be overcome with the continued and vivid realization and declaration that plenty and order are the everlasting facts of being, and that there are no contrary facts. All that appears to the contrary is not fact, but destructible illusion.

The affairs of mortals, both mental and physical, often get into sad tangles, and grow worse and worse past their power to help; but this is not the case with true Christians. "All things work together for good to them that love God," to them that love Him actively enough to be on the alert to realize and enforce His law, in their own consciousness first, and then outwardly in the circle of their legitimate affairs.

HINDRANCES TO HEALING
(From *The Christian Science Journal* of July, 1909)

Usually it is not difficult for a patient to see that unbelief, lack of understanding, sin, doubt, discouragement, fear, and lack of application tend to retard or prevent healing in Christian Science. But there are hindrances of another class which stand in the way of the desired end, and which are usually more difficult for the patient to discern. These appear in the way solely because the patient has not learned the lesson of what self-surrender means, hence he does not know how to go about it; and this not having been accomplished, the unconscious assertion of self leads him to put many stumbling blocks in his own way.

Jesus said to his disciples: "If any man will come after me, let him deny himself, and take up his cross, and follow me." The self which must be denied or renounced, is the carnal mind which Paul declared is "enmity against God: for it is not subject to the law of God, neither indeed can be." Many people have not carefully thought out these matters, or carefully searched the Scriptures with regard to them. It is this implicit belief that we get into the understanding of the truth and the kingdom of God by commencing where we are, and by correcting, developing, and enlarging that which we already have, until finally we shall reach perfection. Those, however, who act upon this theory make as radical a mistake as did those of ancient times, who thought to start upon the earth as a foundation and build a tower which would reach to heaven. God brought their work to utter confusion and destruction, as He does with the work of those who try to build spiritual life, or to gain spiritual health, on the basis of the carnal mind.

Said the apostle: "Other foundation can no man lay than that is laid, which is Jesus Christ;" and in immediate connection with this declaration we also find these words: "Let no man deceive himself. If any man among you seemeth to be wise in this world, let him become a fool, that he may be wise. For the wisdom of this world is foolishness with God." The fact is, that before we can learn much of the saving truth, we must be willing and ready to discard, as having no truth, reliability, or permanent value, all of that habit of thought and all of our so-called knowledge which is directly or indirectly based on the body or the testimony of the senses. In the measure that we have emptied our minds of "philosophy and vain deceit, after the tradition of men, after the rudiments of the world," we are ready to learn and experience the benefits of Truth. Said Jesus: "Except ye be converted, and become as little children, ye shall not enter into the kingdom of heaven. Whosoever therefore shall humble himself as this little child, the same is greatest in the kingdom of heaven." Jesus said again: "No man can come to me, except the Father which hath sent me draw him;" that is, we cannot bring our mortal selves, our carnal minds, to God. We must renounce, or give up, the carnal mind, and let the Spirit be manifested in us; and thus we come to Christ.

Self not having been renounced, it crops out in various ways, to the hindrance of the demonstration of Truth and of the patient's progress. Some of these ways, we do well to consider, not for the purpose of condemning those who have been ignorant that they were transgressing the law of Spirit, but for the purpose of helping all to uncover and recognize the error, so that we may turn away from it and follow in the true way. Most people, when they turn to Truth for help, do so, not because they care about Truth, but because they care about themselves They want God's help, if He has any to bestow; but it may not even occur to them that they are to make any sacrifice therefor, except the payment of some money to a practitioner, and the giving up of some of their time to reading under the practitioner's direction. At the start they do not know that Truth requires of them to gain a totally new and different understanding of life and health, and also in some ways to follow after a different manner of life; but after a time they begin to perceive something of what the demands of Truth are, and then comes the test. Will they renounce self as manifested in the former ways of thought and living, and follow after the truth, because it is the truth, irrespective of whether they have already received benefits or not? If so, then they are loyal to the truth, and unless they are placing stumbling-blocks in their own way along some other line, they will be healed in God's own time; for they have fulfilled the condition: "Seek ye first the kingdom of God, and his righteousness; and all these things shall be added unto you."

Many people desire to buy (with as small an expenditure as possible) their health, with the conscious or unconscious purpose to go on living their former lives of worldly pleasure, when health has been attained. The error and disappointment of such people are well described by James: "Ye ask, and receive not, because ye ask amiss, that ye may consume it upon your lusts. Ye adulterers and adulteresses, know ye not that the friendship of the world is enmity with God? whoever therefore will be a friend of the world is the enemy of God... God resisteth the proud, but giveth grace unto the humble. Submit yourselves therefore to God. Resist the devil, and he will flee from you. Draw nigh to God, and he will draw nigh to you... Humble yourselves in the sight of the Lord, and he shall lift you up."

When an individual has the proper appreciation of the healing truth, he will feel toward it as Jesus describes in Matthew's Gospel; "The kingdom of heaven is like unto a merchant man, seeking goodly pearls: who, when he had found one pearl of great price, went and sold all that he had, and bought it." The lesson on this point is further enforced by the teachings of Jesus, when he counseled the rich young man to give up all his possessions and become his follower.

If we have firmly determined to sacrifice all, if necessary, for Truth, very often we shall not be called upon to make the sacrifice; and it is an immense help toward healing to have this point settled in the patient's mind, so that he will not acquire the habit of measuring a benefit received by the money paid out, but will have his mind at rest upon this question, that he may be free to attend to lines of thought which are beneficial instead of detrimental. We are by no means so ready to be healed by Spirit, if we are all the time judging and examining results with the critical disposition of mortal calculation. The thing to do, is to make ready to surrender our all to Spirit, and thus be the better prepared to receive the gifts of Spirit.

  A student who is really interested in his studies does not long for his school days to cease. If he could in any way manage it, he would be glad to spend his time and money to go on in school and college indefinitely, and so in the case of the person who loves music. Likewise, a patient, if he loves the truth for its own sake, will not be in a hurry to get through with his practitioner, if the practitioner is helping him to a higher understanding of Truth. A patient who is not anxious to get out from under his practitioner's care at the earliest possible moment, for the sake of saving time and money, but who takes such a mental attitude that he is always looking for an opportunity to learn more of Truth, for which he is as glad to make return as is the average person for the theater or the excursion, is certain to have healing and all other needed good added unto him.

  There are some who come into a partial understanding of Science, but who say to themselves or others that they are not ready to believe until they have had a sign in demonstration of the truth by being healed, notwithstanding that they know of plenty of signs which have been given in the healing of other people. If a person makes the receiving of a sign the condition of his believing, he seldom gets it. The reason evidently is, that those who would test Truth by outward signs, wish to walk by sight, instead of walking by faith or understanding. They have not surrendered self, or the carnal mind, which wants to test everything by sense testimony. Self, or the carnal mind, is prone to set itself up as a judge, and say to Science: "Come now, pass in review before me, and show your works. If they are satisfactory, I will believe you." But Science may not be reviewed by mortal mind in this fashion. It demands rather that mortal mind, instead of setting itself up to judge, shall completely humble itself, and say: "I am not fit or worthy to know or judge anything."

Several times, people came to Jesus asking for signs in order that they might believe. Jesus gave plenty of signs to those who did not ask for them; but to people who did ask for them he said: "An evil and adulterous generation seeketh after a sign; and there shall no sign be given to it, but the sign of the prophet Jonas." The sign of the prophet Jonas, as given in the Bible story, is this: Jonas was commanded of the Spirit to go to a certain place and do a certain work. Jonas did not respond to the summons obediently, but rather took ship to go in exactly the opposite direction. He was thrown into the sea, swallowed by a whale, and carried back to where he started from, and was told to do that which Spirit commanded. So it will be with every mortal man. In the end, he will be obliged to do that which Truth demands of him; therefore the sooner he does it, the better for him. Jesus did give to doubting Thomas a sign; but, when Thomas expressed his belief because of the sign, Jesus rebuked him, saying: "Thomas, because thou hast seen me, thou hast believed: blessed are they that have not seen, and yet have believed."

Many people, when they are having treatment, make the mistake of saying to themselves or others: "Now I will have treatment so many days, or so many weeks, and then, if I am not healed, I will stop." This is another attempt of the carnal mind (self) to set limits and make conditions for Truth, while Truth demands that the carnal mind shall completely humble itself. Said Jesus: "It is not for you to know the times or the seasons, which the Father hath put in his own power." And again he said: "In such an hour as ye think not the Son of man cometh." If we did not set ourselves up to dictate times and seasons to Spirit, but in humility were to let Spirit have its own way, our mental attitude would be such that we would be healed in days, instead of the weeks consumed under the conditions which we have prescribed. The true mental attitude is this: "Not my will, but thine, be done."

Patients whose healing is somewhat delayed, are often tempted to set themselves up to judge the work of Spirit by comparing their own case with that of some they know who have been healed much more quickly. This disposition is thoroughly rebuked by Jesus in the parable given us in the twentieth chapter of Matthew. All that Christ, Truth, can bestow upon any person is understanding, plenty, holiness, healing, and joy in the Spirit. These are symbolized in the parable by the "penny." It is not for us to complain whether we are required to work for these one hour or twelve hours, twelve days or twelve months. It is our business simply to follow in the way and be faithful.

Neither should we be envious or attempt to judge the situation by the case of those who are healed more quickly than are we. Not infrequently those who are speedily healed do not acquire so clear an understanding of the truth of Science; and if our fuller understanding must come in advance of the healing, we need not complain, but rather rejoice that by any expenditure of time and effort it may be attained. Impatience and haste are great detriments to healing. Many times it is not realized until after the patient has consciously acquired and assimilated an entirely new understanding of life and health. It was so in the writer's case. During many weary weeks, he seemed to receive no apparent benefit from treatment, until he came unto the understanding and acceptance of Christian Science as Jesus taught and practiced it. After he gained this understanding, his healing was rapid and thorough.

Paul tells us: "Be not conformed to this world: but be ye transformed by the renewing of your mind, that ye may prove what is that good, and acceptable, and perfect, will of God." It is only because we are in a false sense of ourselves that we seem to be sick, and we have to be transformed out of this false mind, which conforms to this world's way of thinking, into the Mind of Spirit, which is the Mind of health, joy, strength, peace, and life eternal. To accomplish this transformation is the greatest, most important, and most beneficent task that any human being ever did or ever can undertake; and to attain this transformation in understanding and realization often requires weeks, sometimes months, even years. Suppose it does. Should we not be as willing to spend all the time necessary to gain the understanding of the Science of eternal life, and to gain permanently our health in the process, as we spend money and months of time to learn the science of algebra, astronomy, or chemistry?

The Bible contains many exhortations to be patient and persistent while we are being healed by Spirit, God. Let us read and heed the following as a single example: "For we know that the whole creation groaneth and travaileth in pain together until now. And not only they, but ourselves also, which have the first fruits of the Spirit, even we ourselves groan within ourselves, waiting for the adoption, to wit, the redemption of our body. For we are saved by hope; but hope that is seen is not hope: for what a man seeth, why doth he yet hope for? But if we hope for that we see not, then do we with patience wait for it."

Too often patients unconsciously maintain a spirit of self-righteousness, which acts very much to their own detriment. They may say, "I have done, as nearly as I could, what the practitioner told me, I have paid for my treatment, and I have tried earnestly to avoid committing sin. I do not see why I am not healed." If the patient can truthfully make such an assertion, then perchance but one thing is lacking — namely, self-surrender through love. Without love, we do all these things in a calculating spirit, in a spirit of bargaining, saying to ourselves that because we have done such and such things, therefore we have a right to expect such and such things in return. But love never calculates, never bargains. A lover bestows time and gifts freely upon the object of his affections, looking for nothing in return except her love, and is continually seeking other ways in which he may serve and please. He does not calculate and bargain with her, even in his own thought. Because he approaches her in this way, she, though reserved and hesitant at first, at length comes to the point where she is ready to bestow upon him her unreserved affection.

So if we seek the truth, not because we are looking for what it will bestow, but because we really love it for its own sake and are anxious to spend time and money in acquiring it and serving it, then its riches speedily become our possession. The proper way to seek the truth may be expressed in the following paraphrase: I take thee for better, for worse; for richer, for poorer; in sickness and in health; in prosperity and adversity; to love and to cherish, to have and to hold forever; and upon thee I bestow all my worldly goods. Truth, thus sought, will not long withhold her blessings.

TRUSTING GOD

Except insofar as it prevents fear and worry — which is much, if actually accomplished — it does not do very much good to blindly trust our mortal affairs to God, on the supposition that He orders them and will take care of them. God does not order mortal affairs; for mortal affairs are only a mistaken sense of things. God and His work, and all affairs that He orders, are immortal. God, being immortal, does not make or order anything mortal.

Suppose one had problems in mathematics to work, and should say: "Well, I will trust the principle of mathematics to work out these problems." It is true, that such problems can only be worked out by the principle of mathematics; *yet the person desiring the solution of a problem has something to do in the matter.* He must *understand* mathematics, and *apply* that understanding, in order to solve his problem; or he must have his problems solved by someone else who understands mathematics, and will apply that understanding for him.

Likewise, in order to overcome ills, a man must *understand* God and consciously *apply* his understanding in order to overcome these ills; or he must have them overcome for him by someone else who understands God, and will apply that understanding in his behalf, else the ills will not be overcome. No amount of blind trust will remove them; neither will they be removed by prayers or petitions to a supposed God, who is supposed to have established these ills, waiting for someone to pray to Him before He will remove them. There is no such God.

Christian Science teaches us *how to understand* God; and how to *apply our understanding* to the present overcoming of sin, disease, discord, and poverty; and, sometime, either in this or some future stage of growth, our increased understanding of God will enable us to permanently overcome our sense of materiality and death.

The fact that men use the laws of mathematics for the solution of many problems shows that they are entirely sure that the correct application of these laws will bring correct and useful results, and they evidence their trust in these laws by learning them and using them intelligently; not by relying on them while yet remaining in ignorance of them.

The trust in God which is effectual in results, requires not only a thorough comprehension and detailed knowledge of the laws of God, but a practical, available knowledge of them. To illustrate: Before a boy can learn the multiplication table to any purpose, such expressions as: "Three times four equals twelve," "Five times six equals thirty," and so on, must be illustrated to him, so that he clearly understands their meaning. Then he must commit to memory these expressions arranged in tables. This requires much close application, much concentration of thought, and much repetition and drill on his part; but even after he has mastered the tables so that he can recite them glibly, he still lacks a knowledge of them that can be put to much practical use. For instance, suppose the boy is given a problem, to multiply 465 by 23. When he is confronted by the demand that he multiply five by three, he may not know the result, except as he has learned it by rote in the table; so he must go through a process, as follows: "Three times one are three, three times two are six, etc.," until he reaches "three times five are fifteen." By this process, he is able to reach the truth he seeks; but he has not yet acquired independent knowledge of it.

Suppose that, at the point where the boy knows his addition, subtraction and multiplication tables by rote, he is sent to the market to buy six oranges at three cents each, and with a quarter of a dollar to pay for them; and suppose the clerk who makes the change is inclined to be dishonest, and gives the boy four cents in change, instead of seven. The boy, not being familiar with the mathematical reasoning involved, is likely to be confused by the situation. He indistinctly perceives that he has not been given enough change, and yet his knowledge of the facts is not instant and ready-on-demand. He timidly suggests to the clerk that he has not been given the right change, and the clerk, assuming a bold air, replies: "Yes, your change is all right."

"But, but —," ventures the boy.

"Run along, I tell you; your change is all right," blusters the clerk, and, not being sufficiently sure of his ground to make a stand, the boy goes away defrauded.

If the boy had acquired an independent command of the problem, then, when the clerk undertook to cheat him, a look of surprise would instantly and automatically have come into his face, and that, in all probability, would have shown the clerk that his purpose to defraud was useless, and he would have said: "Oh, excuse me, I did not give you the right change." But if the clerk had tried to hold his ground, with what absolute and positive assurance would the boy have claimed his right! He would have stood for his due until he got it. An instantly available knowledge of the truth would have protected him against the imposition.

So, too, when we have learned what the laws of God are, and thoroughly drilled them into our consciousness by meditation, declaration, and application, then when any suggestion from within or without contrary to those laws arises, we are instantly surprised that there should be even a presumption that any thought or circumstance could successfully assert or carry through anything contrary to the laws of God. We are then protected against suffering and loss, as we never can be by any degree of knowledge less thoroughly assimilated in consciousness.

It is therefore often useful for a person to declare and endeavor to realize, many times each day, that love, joy, peace, and confidence in good are laws of God, and therefore of our being; that whenever we tolerate fear, anxiety, worry, doubt, or grief, we are breaking the law, and living a lie: that harmony, health, strength, action, life, express the laws of God, and that whenever we tolerate, without protest, thoughts or feelings of sickness, pain, weakness, inaction, or death, we are breaking the law, and living a lie. He who thus drills right thoughts into his consciousness, until they are brought into the very forefront of thought, and so cannot be forgotten when they are needed, and who orders his course in accordance with divine law, will be subject to very little suffering, either mental or physical, and to very little loss in any way.

REJOICING IN TRIBULATION

A Christian man once said to a friend, "I do not believe that there is anyone in this city who feels richer than I do, today." "Why," the friend inquired, "what makes you feel that way?" "My feeling arises in connection with a financial difficulty," was the reply. "My rent has not been paid for the last two months." "I do not see how you can feel rich over that," said the surprised friend. "I should think that you would feel quite the contrary." "Yes," answered the man, "I supposed you would think so. I know that you have been worrying over the condition of your business affairs, and that is why I made this remark to you, with the purpose of explaining my reasons for feeling rich under the circumstances that I have named, although I certainly would avoid debt when possible, and I am not ignoring the rights of the landlord, of which I shall speak later." Then the speaker went on talking, somewhat as follows:

In the Scriptures, we are exhorted to become "rich toward God," to "lay up for ourselves treasures in heaven," and to "seek first the kingdom of God, and His righteousness." The Bible gives us to understand that the only true riches are spiritual riches, riches of consciousness, which are to be gained from God alone. All men are seeking what they call "happiness;" but few know of what it really consists, or how to find it. Happiness can be nothing else than desirable states of consciousness; and the only desirable states of consciousness, on which it is possible to gain a lasting hold, are those which are based upon the realization of God and His manifestation in the mentalities of men. God is the only creator, the only power, the only governor, the only law-maker. God is everywhere present, and, according to His nature, is always manifest as love, joy, and peace. Hence, love, joy, and peace, are the law of the universe, the law of being, the law of every man's mentality. When, therefore, a man realizes love, joy and peace as proceeding from God, and as being based upon Him, rather than as proceeding from material things or human beings, he is truly living; but when a man entertains fear, doubt, grief, anxiety, foreboding, or any mental state contrary to love, joy, peace, and confidence in good, he is breaking the law of his being, and is living a lie; that is, he really is not living at all, since false life is not life. There is no actual life which is not a manifestation of God, which does not express love, peace, and joy. Any other seeming life is only a counterfeit, an appearance which is not real. If we would really live, we must manifest or reflect God.

Love, joy and peace which we think we have because of a hold upon certain material possessions, or because of relations socially agreeable, though non-spiritual, with certain people, are not the genuine article; they are counterfeit; they rest upon the wrong foundation. But love, joy, and peace, which we know to be based upon God, and which we hold because we are conscious of right relations with Him, these are the desirable states of consciousness which constitute the only true riches. Such riches are "the pearl of great price"; and, to gain them, it is worth a man's while to part with everything else that he has, if necessary.

It is the habit of most people to seek for love, joy, and peace from outward circumstances and from people, and not from God. Humanly speaking, men do not come naturally by spiritual riches, any more than they come naturally by mathematics or a musical education. The true riches have to be laboriously gained, just as everything worth having in this human world has to be gained. Indeed, it is as unnatural for the carnal man to live in spiritual consciousness, and thus to be spiritually rich, as it is for him to live in water. Men can learn to support themselves in water, and to live in water a considerable portion of the time; and likewise, they can learn to live in Spirit a great deal of the time, and to enjoy themselves in spiritual life, independently, for the most part, of what is going on in matter or among people. The following illustration may help us to understand more clearly the process which we must go through in learning to live the spiritual life, and thus to be truly rich.

Suppose a boy has set his heart upon learning to swim. He will do well to commence practicing in comparatively shallow water. For a time, he should remain where he can put his feet down and touch bottom at any time, without being over his head. But he will never be satisfied with himself as a swimmer until he has attained the ability to go out into deep water, and remain there an hour at a time. He should not go into deep water too soon; but when he finds himself swimming in deep water, he does not lament, but rejoices. After remaining out of touch with the ground for a time, supported by the water only, he returns to land; but, even while living on land, he can have the satisfaction of knowing that he is a swimmer worthy of the name. To remain such, he must, of course, spend considerable time in the water and keep in practice.

A man who sets out to attain life in and of Spirit cannot learn to support himself in spiritual consciousness all at once, any more than he can learn to swim all at once. He must begin by learning to depend on Spirit somewhat, a little more each week and month that passes, and to depend correspondingly less and less upon things and upon people for his happiness. Thus, as he grows spiritually, the time will come when he can maintain peace and joy in consciousness with practically no material means of support in sight; and when a person of any considerable length of experience in the Christian life finds himself in such a situation, instead of being anxious, grieved, or frightened about it, he should simply say to himself: "The material foundations for peace, joy, and confidence, on which I have been accustomed to depend, are now, for the time being, out of my reach; I am in the deep water of Spirit. I wonder if, now, I cannot so depend upon Spirit, God, that I can maintain confidence, peace, and joy on the basis of my realizing the presence of spiritual good. A man of my religious experience should not look upon this present withdrawal of material support as a calamity, but should regard it as a testing time, by which I may ascertain how strong my confidence in God really is; and, if I find that I can maintain my hold on joy, with little or no material occasion for joy in sight, but with outward temptations to the contrary, I should rejoice in my present situation, as much as does the boy who has desired to learn to swim, when he finds himself swimming with confidence and success in deep water."

A man can never really know whether he is a good swimmer or not, so long as his feet are on the bottom. Likewise, a man can never really know whether he is strong in Spirit, if he has never been tried by having human and material foundations for confidence swept away from him. But after a man has been through such an experience, after he has been in deep water with God, and has found that he can maintain the life of peace and joy in spite of material lack, then he may return again to a condition of material plenty; but, even when dwelling in the midst of material abundance, much as he did before, he does so with a different consciousness. He knows that he can live by Spirit, if necessary, as he did not know before. He can say with Paul: "I have learned both how to abound, and how to suffer lack."

In the spiritual growth of each one of us, it seems almost necessary that, at some time, we shall be put through a testing time; and, usually, the testing time comes. If we measure up to the test, if, instead of whining, lamenting, and being afraid, we fall back on our knowledge and realization of God and His manifestations, and determine to be happy anyway, even more so because the time for us to be worthy to be tested has arrived — then it invariably happens that, before very long, the usual supply of human comforts are restored to us; but if we do not prove that we can live in peace and joy alone with God, we will be forced to endure a continuance of material lack, or recurring experiences of it, until we do learn the spiritual lesson of being happy in spiritual possessions only. There seems to be no way of escaping such a testing time; and it is probably essential to our spiritual growth that there should be no way of escape, until we have learned the requisite lesson, and thus learn the meaning of St. Paul's experience of "rejoicing in tribulation."

It is from a standpoint of realization such as this, to a large extent, that the withdrawal of one's material means of supply can be to him a distinct occasion for feeling rich — rich in the realization of spiritual good, which constitutes the only true riches.

But the question may be raised: "How about the landlord, from whom the rent was being withheld? Suppose that he might be needing it. What is to be said from his point of view?" The reply is that, of course, his tenant should pay the rent if he could, and, without doubt, should do so. If he could not, it would not help the situation in the least for him to worry, fret, or be afraid of anything; for him to lapse into such a state of mind, would becloud his intelligence, sap his strength, and thus tend to prevent his gaining the means to pay the rent.

"But does God provide a testing time for the real, spiritual advantage of one of His children at the expense of what seems like the just due of another?" No, "God is no respecter of persons." "God is light, and in Him is no darkness at all." God creates only absolute good, and dwells in the consciousness of nothing but absolute good. He is immortal, and does not create His opposite. He neither creates nor orders material affairs. Men are in darkness, and only reach light as they work their way into a consciousness of God. "The natural man receiveth not the things of the spirit of God; for they are spiritually discerned." If a landlord has sufficiently learned his spiritual lesson respecting the working out of humanity's problem, he will not be the one at whose seeming expense the spiritual growth of another will be promoted; but, if he has not learned to "live in the Spirit and walk in the Spirit," then he also needs the experience of being made to suffer material lack, until he too wakes up and learns his spiritual lesson.

Let us try to describe, at its best, the life which is merely or mostly human. A boy is born and reared in a good family. He goes to school and college, and is diligent and studious. He keeps the moral law, and lives above reproach among his fellow men. He marries a girl of excellent family, education, character and refinement. They have children who are the admiration of all who know them. Before marrying, the man started in business. He was and is intelligent and capable. From the start, he makes a good living. His debts are always paid on the day they are due. He has a reputation to be proud of in the business world, and is proud of it. Men say of him: "His word is as good as his bond." He can borrow a reasonable amount of money at any bank, because he is known to be successful and honest and to have accumulated some resources. He and the members of his family attend church regularly as a matter of course, and support the church liberally. They all move in the most intelligent and refined social circles.

      Now, all of this may be, and sometimes is, what John disapprovingly speaks of as, "the pride of life," in the following text: "Love not the world, neither the things that are in the world; for if any man love the world, the love of the Father is not in him; for all that is in the world, the lust of the flesh, and the lust of the eyes, and the pride of life, are not of the Father, but of the world. And the world passeth away, and the lust thereof; but he that doeth the will of God abideth forever." The man, whom we have described, would doubtless think of himself, if asked about it, as a godly man; but he has never closely analyzed his own thought. As a matter of fact, so far as he thinks about it at all, he has an implicit sense that he is good, that he is honest and upright, that he is diligent and intelligent, that he has made a business and social position for himself, that he has accumulated property and made a place in the world, that he is secure in the good place which he has made. If so, his sense of security, peace and joy all rest on a false, material, and human foundation, which, very likely, may have to be swept from under his feet in order that he may wake up to what is the true foundation for security and joy — namely, the knowledge of Spirit, God, and not material goods and the good opinion of men. The man has not yet learned the significance of the words of Jesus: "Why callest thou me good? There is none good, save one, that is God." He has not yet taken to heart the scripture which says: "Trust in the Lord with all thy heart, and lean not to thine own understanding; but in all thy ways acknowledge Him, and He shall direct thy paths."

But after such a man has successfully experienced his testing time (and fortunate is he who promptly recognizes the opportunity for a test, and its significance, when it comes), and has proved that he can live in joy without any special amount of worldly goods or human approval, then, very likely, all the outward possessions that he had before will be given back to him in multiplied measure; but let him beware of again allowing his heart to trust in his material riches. Let him continue to be diligent to "lay up treasures in heaven [in spiritual consciousness] where moth and rust do not corrupt, and where thieves do not break through and steal."

* * * * * * *

EVIL HATH NO ORIGIN

God, the infinite good, created all that is, and good never created its opposite, any more than light could create darkness. Therefore evil is not created, and does not belong to reality. It is an appearance without foundation in fact; therefore an illusion; therefore no thing, nothing.

When did truth become a lie? The answer is, Truth did not become a lie. When did evil, illusion, nothing, begin? The answer is, evil, no thing, nothing, did not begin.

Philosophizing about the origin of nothing has consumed such an amount of time and effort that, had they been spent in contemplation of the Truth which heals, much more of health and good would have been demonstrated.

All sins and evils are mistakes. God never makes mistakes. Hence mortal mind makes its own mistakes, and God is not the author of sin or evil.

THE RIGHTEOUSNESS WHICH IS BY FAITH

"Righteousness" was formerly spelled "right-wisness" (right-wise-ness). It means, fundamentally, a right sense, including right understanding and right feeling. It is, first of all, a condition of consciousness, and only secondarily a matter of outward conduct.

Faith, in the Scriptural sense, is not synonymous in meaning with the word *trust*. Its meaning is better conveyed in the terms *God-consciousness* or *spiritual discernment*. In *Science and Health*, Mrs. Eddy says, "Spiritual sense is a conscious, constant capacity to understand God." The phrase, "The righteousness which is by faith," might well be paraphrased by the words, "The right sense which is, in fact, God-consciousness."

It is impossible to correctly sense anything except as we do so through its qualities, manifestations, or attributes. For instance, we might hear about gold as a name, but we can only sense it through yellowness, hardness, opacity, etc. Likewise, we can hear about God as a name; but if we sense God, we shall only do so as we sense love, joy, peace, strength, harmony, liberty, and the other constant, changeless manifestations of God. In the case of gold, we do not immediately and necessarily sense some of its qualities, such as malleability and ductility, though, as just stated, we cannot fail to sense the qualities yellowness, hardness and opacity, if we sense gold at all. So, in apprehending God, we do not necessarily, at first, sense Him as strength, harmony, health, liberty, life; but we cannot apprehend Him at all unless we sense Him as love, joy, and peace. And God is thus felt, if at all, by a direct mental contact. He is as definitely felt mentally as is a piece of velvet or the petal of a rose physically. We do not get a realization of the God-love, the God-joy, the God-peace, the God-strength, the God-liberty, etc., through things or people, but only inwardly; it is the love, the joy, the peace, the honesty, the truthfulness, the strength, the harmony, the liberty, the life, which are inwardly sensed as unfailing, changeless attributes of God, that constitute "the righteousness which is by faith." The qualities so named which rest on a mortal or material basis, are counterfeit and unreliable, and it is worth while to illustrate and examine why this is so.

    Suppose one human being loves another, and then the other one dies or removes to a distance. Immediately, the joy of human love largely changes to, or is replaced by, grief. If the one loved does not reciprocate, but bestows his love on a third party, then human love may become the occasion of jealousy. If the one loved becomes seriously ill, human love occasions fear. The one loved pursues certain lines of action, then human love changes to, or is replaced by, hatred. But our sense of divine Love, if we have it, "never faileth." This is because our possession of spiritual love rests between us and God alone, and He never changes, and we do not need to change in our sense of Him, whatever goes on in the world of matter and people. In a family which had gotten into financial difficulties for the first time, the lady said lamentingly, that it seemed so queer for them to be in such a situation; that in the twenty years of their married life, there had never before been a time that they could not lie down at night with the thought that they owed no man a dollar; and that she supposed she ought to be thankful for their twenty years of peace instead of mourning over present troubles, since most people had far more. As a matter of fact, her twenty years of peace on a material basis amounted to nothing for true and lasting gain. It was only counterfeit peace. Had it been genuine — the peace which pertains to God-consciousness — it would have stood the test in this time of perplexity. Indeed, had the family had the righteousness which is by faith, probably they would have had the wisdom to have avoided this business disaster altogether.

    As a younger man, the author, though engaged in religious work, could not understand why the honesty of an irreligious man, who told the truth, kept his promises, and paid his debts, was not just as good as any other honesty, and, indeed, why it did not exemplify the only kind of honesty there is. It is now easy to see that the honesty of the world is of "the best policy" type, that it is evolved from experience, or is an imitation of that honesty which is in the world from a truly religious source. This worldly honesty, though doubtless better than dishonesty, is only counterfeit, and will not endure without breaking the test of hard experience, as does the honesty which is by God-consciousness.

Christian Science enables one to perceive that there are many professors of Christian faith who, nevertheless, have really little if any of the righteousness which is by faith. They suppose themselves to have it, but are deceived because they do not really understand what faith is, thinking it to be belief in some creed or "scheme of salvation," or "belief in Christ" in a sense different than the *understanding* of Christ and the application of his law. Such righteousness does not differ materially from the righteousness of the world, which is on a "natural" basis — and of which Paul wrote, "The natural man receiveth not things of the spirit of God."

It should not be difficult to discern that the strength, harmony, and liberty of body and mind which are the fruitage of God-consciousness, are from a different source, and rest on a different basis than the so-called strength, health, and liberty which seem to be conditions of the body itself, when in its normal, natural state. These latter are but imitations of the genuine, and do not endure the test of strain and stress.

The purity which is gained through the apprehension of Love is immeasurably stronger to endure temptation than is "natural" purity; indeed, one having a strong realization of faith-purity is scarcely susceptible of being strongly tempted. The prince of this world cometh and findeth nothing in him, in the way of impurity; and so it is in all lines for him who has thoroughly acquired "the righteousness which is by faith." This righteousness, instead of failing in time of difficulty, comes into more vigorous action, and shines with greater brilliance.

The Righteousness Which Is by Faith

"I counsel thee," says the Revelator, "to buy of me gold tried in the fire, that thou mayest be rich; and white raiment that thou mayest be clothed, and that the shame of thy nakedness do not appear." He who has "the righteousness which is by faith," has this "gold tried in the fire," and does not object to its being fire tested. As a mathematician grows skillful by the problems which he works upon and solves, and not by those which he avoids, so the God-conscious man knows that he becomes spiritually and joyfully rich, not by the human difficulties which he avoids, but by those which he faces, works upon — long and hard, if need be — and solves by the knowledge and power of God; and the harder the problem, the greater the joy in working on it, and the greater the gain in solving it. The righteousness which is by faith enables a man to regard difficulties, not as an annoyance and a burden, but as a great opportunity. They furnish the fire in which he may refine his gold, and so become rich indeed. Dealing with them, he "rejoiceth as a strong man to run a race."

While working on hard situations, the faith-righteous man never thinks of tolerating doubt, fear, foreboding, anger, envy or grief. His feelings are stayed on God, and he knows that he is far better off than those who are reposing in worldly ease and worldly harmony, for "the friendship of the world is enmity with God," and enmity with spiritual joy. "The kingdom of God consisteth not in meat and drink [and other human riches], but in righteousness [God-consciousness], peace and joy in the Holy Spirit." Says the poet:

> *One ship sails east, another west,*
> *By the self-same winds that blow:*
> *'Tis the set of the sails, and not the gales*
> *That shows us our way to go.*
> *Like the winds of the sea on the waves of fate,*
> *As we voyage on through life,*
> *'Tis the set of the soul that decides the goal,*
> *And not the winds or the strife.*

Most people have too much human pride and too little of what might be termed spiritual pride, that attitude which Jesus defined when he said: "If I honor myself, my honor is nothing. It is my Father that honoreth me." He exemplified it, when as a carpenter's son from the despised village of Nazareth, without money and without a home, he stood before the scribes and Pharisees, the rulers of his people, rich, high born, moral in human and ecclesiastical righteousness, and called them hypocrites and liars to their faces, and told them, "Ye are of your father, the devil, and the lusts of your father, ye will do." Jesus again exemplified the true self-exaltation when he washed his disciples' feet, and said, "He that is greatest among you, let him be your servant." In a given company, he that has the most correct and practical knowledge of God outranks all others, regardless of their wealth, culture, social station, lineage, political or ecclesiastical rank. He may rebuke his world superiors if occasion requires, but will not shrink from serving the humblest who may be in need of service. He who has spiritual self-respect (which is, indeed, God-respect) will unhesitatingly appeal to the highest court of authority, even to God, when called to the bar of public judgment — and he cannot do less if he would honor the Father whom he represents. A writer in *Zion's Herald*, as quoted in *The Christian Science Journal*, truly says: "The one thing greater than human speech is silence. The silence of Christ in the presence of falsehood and detraction was Godlike. In the presence of criticism and exposure, vice can ill afford to close its lips; its hope lies in the witchery and deception of speech. Virtue, on the other hand, can afford to be still, for the reason that there is no wrong to be concealed." Spiritual pride (which is identical with spiritual humility) may explain its actions for the sake of friendship, or for the sake of helping the world at large, or for the sake of maintaining unity of action among those working for a common end.

Human pride glories in a distinguished ancestry, in wealth, culture, noted world achievements, political or ecclesiastical preferment, social eminence, and conventional righteousness — some of which are well enough, and even desirable in their place. Nevertheless the humanly proud might be thrown into a panic at the prospect of financial bankruptcy, while totally indifferent to the fact that they had never been spiritually solvent, had never been prepared to pay to God, on demand, in season or out of season, the unbroken purity, peace and joy in Him which are His constant due, and which every man is spiritually honor-bound to continually exemplify before his fellow men. The servants of human pride would be ashamed not to appear in what they consider suitable dress; yet, on even slight occasion, they have been known to expose their mental nakedness, which is made evident in their fretfulness, fear, anger, jealousy, doubt, grief, etc. Human pride is not ashamed of its lack of "white raiment," the only true clothing.

He who would attain faith-righteousness, must, first of all, perceive the difference between it and "natural" righteousness. After that, the deepening and broadening of the direct, inner sense of mental contact with God is a matter of growth through experience, and especially, perhaps, through trials and difficulties. This God-consciousness, coming in little by little, transforms the mentality, gradually crowds out all sin and sickness, and brings the aspiring Christian to a progressive experience in which, more and more, whatever the vicissitudes of life, he "rejoices with joy unspeakable and full of glory."

* * * * * * *

If hazards of false teachings and mistaken ideals multiply, the need of the church is not to rear higher its external defenses, but most solemnly to renew its reliance on the invincible and infallible spiritual leadership of the Master who dwells within it. When the presence of Jesus Christ in the church seems less potent for its protection than measures of ecclesiastical authority, the mood cries to heaven for a livelier realization of Jesus Christ. *Anon*

DEALING WITH MALPRACTICE
(A letter to a patient)

Dear Friend:

Your letter of January 15th suggests a subject of large proportions. It suggests the application or use of truth, as made known through Christian Science, in dealing with and destroying error. It is quite a task to get a clear and comprehensive knowledge of truth, yet it is a far more difficult task to learn how to uncover error in all its phases, and how to apply truth wisely, so as to destroy error. Truth is fixed and invariable, being all logically deducible from its Principle, God. Therefore it is possible to gain an exact knowledge of truth, and it is comparatively easy for a thoroughly logical mind to do so. But error, the devil, is a liar. It has no principle, and is never logically harmonious with itself, except when it suits its own purposes to be so. When we have learned a manifestation of Truth we have learned it, that is all there is to it; but when we think we have a manifestation of error located and cornered, likely as not, unless wisely handled, the devil will bring forth another lie in the place of the one we have destroyed, not exactly the same lie, but one just as troublesome; and we find ourselves, if we are not wise, engaged in the endless process of "chasing the devil around a stump." Because of its false, unstable, changeable character, error is vastly more complex, and in a way, harder to get at than truth. If we could learn how to uncover and destroy error as quickly as we grasp a theoretical knowledge of Science, the whole false sense of the universe would have been destroyed long ago.

The knowledge of theoretical Christian Science means much, and many attain unto this in large measure; but the knowledge how wisely to uncover and destroy error, is also sure to distinguish a successful Christian Scientist from one who is not. Scientists may have a good theoretical understanding of truth; but when they attempt to handle and destroy error, they are likely to simply stir up and multiply its manifestations, if they are not "wise as serpents, and harmless as doves."

Malpractice is wrong thinking, thinking contrary to the Science of Truth. For instance, if one should think, "The paper says, 'A storm will come tomorrow' and I am liable to have rheumatism," this is malpractice, because it is wrong thinking. It attributes power to supposed conditions of weather which are not real, and assumes that something other than God, good, has power over man. Suppose, however, one should think as follows: "The paper says that a storm will come on tomorrow, and mortal mind will be trying to convince me that I must have rheumatism as a result; but I know that mortal mind is a liar. It has no power, since God is the only power. Neither it, nor any so-called material conditions have control over me, while I abide 'in the secret place of the most High!' God is not the author of rheumatism, and His child cannot be afflicted with it." This is not mental malpractice; it is foreseeing what error will try to assert, and is attempting to destroy the error before it can make its assertion. If the attempt is successful, the error is met.

If you see a person who is thinly clad, sitting beside an open window, and you think, "I am afraid he will take cold," that is malpractice. But if you think, "Man dwelling in the atmosphere of Truth and Love, which is the only real atmosphere, cannot take cold, since mortal mind and its conditions have no power over him," this is not malpractice; it is a declaration of truth which is protective and remedial.

If a superintendent of a Sunday school, who understands both Christian Science and the methods of error, were to transfer a child of Mrs. S. from one class of the Sunday school to another, he might think, from his general knowledge of the ways of evil, that it would be likely to suggest to Mrs. S. that this change was made from some sinister motive — not that he would think of Mrs. S. as more suspicious than most mortals, but he would remember that we are all very human, and still open to suggestions of the common enemy, when off our guard. He would not know positively that evil would make such suggestion to Mrs. S., since it is not sure to observe any uniform procedure; but he would know that it always seems to be on the watch for an opportunity to make trouble. To head off any possible working of this one evil, he would do well to declare for the reign of Truth and Love. He might make some such declaration as follows: "This change is intended for the good of this child, and for the good of all concerned. Error has no power to mislead us or anyone else about this matter, or to argue to anyone any misunderstanding of our motives, or to produce any evil in any way. Only the one Mind can guide and govern." Such a mental declaration may prevent error from sowing seeds of discord, which it otherwise would. The mother might not know the reasons for which the change was made, but the love and right thought expressed mentally in making the argument would protect her thought, so that she would feel that everything was done for the best, whether she understood or not.

As the result of our mortal habits of thought, we are constantly disposed to forebode evil for ourselves and for our neighbors in one way or another. This is all malpractice, and we need to be ever on the guard against it. Sometimes we think along these lines, and know that our thought processes are unscientific; yet we are tempted to entertain them, or we are too indolent to make the necessary effort to cast them out. This is conscious mental malpractice. There are people who deliberately send out mental suggestions of disease or disaster to others whom they may hate, or who let jealousy against a given person inflame their consciousness, doing so in the belief that this may bring disease or other disasters on that person. This is malicious mental malpractice, or malicious animal magnetism. Attention can not be too strongly called to the fact that malicious malpractice is wholly powerless to harm one living in the active consciousness of protection in the one divine Mind.

If there are mistakes in the computations of a set of bank books, these mistakes must be sought out and corrected, and the seeking must continue until they are all corrected. It will not be sufficient to make a general assertion that the true result of every possible combination of numbers is already established in mathematical law, and trust this general declaration to correct the mistakes. In the bookkeeping of ordinary daily life, there are many false entries. We know very well that mortal mind, error, is constantly arguing, through the consciousness of mortals on every side of us, skepticism, fear, doubt, foreboding, anger, hatred, malice, envy, jealousy, revenge, agnosticism, materiality, sensuality, intemperance, dishonesty, falsehood, hypnotism, thought transference, spiritualism, etc. — all these errors spring up in the minds of mortals, because the seed is sown there by error, the one evil. All these are manifestations of error, and are unreal, but their unreality is to be proven. They are mistakes in mortal mind which must be corrected, and for this purpose it is often not sufficient to make a general declaration that God is good, and that He made all that was made, and that there can be no evil. When this declaration can be made clearly enough to destroy the manifestations of error, well and good. But if not, then those manifestations must be dealt with and met specifically. Hence, a well instructed Christian Scientist may make such daily declarations of the truth of being as will cover the specific possibilities of error's claim and activity; and when all mankind begin to meet these errors daily with realizations and declarations of truth, they will soon cease to be manifested.

There are segregations of error which may be named *materia medica*, false theology, etc. Error is liable to try to attack a Scientist, or a person coming into Science, through one or more of these segregations of error as a channel. Hence, the Scientist should wisely deal with all these claims in his daily declarations of truth.

Note: This article is not presented as a complete discussion of the subject of "Dealing with Malpractice." It is merely what it purports to be; some thoughts on the subject presented in a letter to a patient.

* * * * * * *

To forbid a man in advance to speak, on the assumption that he may say something illegal, endangers the republic.
Harris Weinstock.

Growth is restricted by forcing humanity out of the proper channels for development or by holding it in fetters.
Mary Baker Eddy

GOD-CONSCIOUSNESS VERSUS SUB-CONSCIOUSNESS

The analysis of the errors with which all human beings have to deal, is often of great practical importance, since it enables us the more intelligently to apply our knowledge of God in their correction. As Mrs. Eddy says in *Science and Health*, "A knowledge of error and its operations must precede that understanding of truth which destroys error."

The organs of the human body are not self-controlled. If they were, the organs of a corpse would be self-acting. It is also evident, that the organs of the body are not under the control of the conscious mind; for the beating of the heart, the digestion of food, and other so-called involuntary bodily processes, go on without any seeming dependence upon our conscious mentality. Furthermore, it is clear to students of Christian Science, that God does not create, nor directly or consciously, attend to the activities of the material body. Nevertheless the activities of the bodily organs evidence intelligence and plan of an intricate and complex order. Since this intelligence is evidently not an expression of the divine consciousness (though Christian Scientists know it to be a counterfeit of God-intelligence), and since it is not conscious human intelligence, the intelligence which controls the bodily organs and functions is spoken of by students of the human mind as "sub-consciousness," — indicating that its activities are beneath the activity or observation of the conscious mind.

The so-called sub-conscious mind is a part of the make-up of every human being, though most human beings give little or no thought to its existence, or to the nature and laws of its activity on the human plane. Furthermore, it has been discovered that the sub-conscious mind gradually takes its character from the activity of the conscious mind. The conscious mind is, as it were, a feeder of the sub-consciousness, which accumulates and stores up that which it is fed; thus it becomes the seat of what is called *habit*, along many different lines. There is an Eastern proverb, said to be thousands of years old, which reads, "If a man commits a sin, let him not do it again; let him not delight in it; the accumulation of evil is painful."

It is fair to say that the sub-consciousness of a young child is largely formed and determined by the belief of inheritance from human ancestors, and by pre-natal influences of the mother's thought and feeling. As the child grows older, its own conscious mental activity, and its mental environment, enter more and more largely into the shaping of its sub-consciousness. Accordingly, it is apparent that the sub-consciousness of an adult is partly the result of the belief of inheritance, partly the result of mental environment, and largely the result of daily conscious activity.

If the conscious mind, to a large extent, entertains fear, anxiety, doubt, grief, discouragement, lust, greed, hatred, malice, envy, jealousy, revenge, pride, and the like, the sub-consciousness becomes habitually discordant; and, if so, sooner or later this discord is manifest in the disease of one or more of the bodily organs or functions which it controls.

Let us examine this mental process a little more carefully. Frequently the conscious mind becomes discordant over business or social experiences, or over some condition of ill-health. This gradually makes the sub-consciousness discordant, which, in turn, manifests itself in disease of the body — and in increased measure, if disease was the original occasion of discord. As a result of this added sense of disease, the conscious mind takes on an increased sense of fear, anxiety, discouragement, grief, etc. This is communicated to the sub-consciousness, thus making it still more discordant, and such a mental descent once entered upon, nothing but extreme suffering and death can result, unless a way is found to interrupt its course.

God-Consciousness vs Sub-Consciousness

We learn in Christian Science that the one sure and legitimate way of stopping this destructive mental program is to lay hold on God, to govern the feelings according to Love, and thus escape from the influence and control of outward or corporeal suggestions of discord. We may not be able to do this all at once; but, with a clear understanding of spiritual truth and firm determination, we can do a great deal in the right direction from the very start, and can soon gain a complete victory. Said Paul, "I can do all things through Christ which strengtheneth me."

It may be well to consider somewhat in detail how we may make a beginning of right activity. First of all, we must be thoroughly convinced that God is the only cause and creator, hence the only power; that anything which seems to occur as the result of any other so-called power cannot be legitimate or real; that the human mind can have no true or real thoughts or feelings which it does not receive from God. Said Christ Jesus: "The son can do [think or feel] nothing of himself; but whatsoever he seeth the Father do [think or feel], that doeth the son likewise." If we clearly perceive and accept this fact, we will determine not to allow ourselves to feel contrary to the nature of God, since, in doing so, we would manifestly be living (feeling) a lie.

To illustrate, suppose a person were to find himself seriously ill. At once the disposition to fear and to worry asserts itself; but he who has awakened to the truth of being, reminds himself that he has accepted God as the only power. In God there is no reason for fear; hence the apparent physical reasons for it are really no reasons at all, and are not to be allowed to govern one, even though he does feel sick. He may for the present be unable to avoid a sense of weakness and pain, though he valiantly contends against them; but, in any case, he will not give place to fear. Such conscious activity, based on divine Love, will tend strongly to prevent the development of disease, and if the realization of spiritual Truth, its law and power, is sufficiently clear, the disease will be destroyed.

In any case, the giving of false suggestions to the sub-consciousness is avoided, and the consequent aggravation of the disease is prevented. Such mental procedure on the part of the Christian Scientist, if it is not sufficient to cure him, will at least aid in his recovery, and will clear the way for effective reception of the work being done for him by a brother Scientist.

Suppose a near relative or friend has passed away. There is a strong "natural" impulsion to grief; but the person who has adopted this new line of activity will at once remember that in God there is no reason for grief; and having accepted this fact, he will not be deceived by appearances, or by what human sense claims to be a reason. Therefore he will not entertain grief. Suppose, to human sense, a dear one should prove "unfaithful." Then comes the "natural" impulsion to jealousy, anger, grief, hatred, revenge, and the like. Again we are reminded that in God there is no reason for any of these feelings, and hence we will not entertain them. We may thus rule out of consciousness all forms of emotional discord, which would ordinarily be incident to business perplexities or reverses, to social relations, to family affairs, or even to the conditions of bodily health.

The person who, by thus accepting God as the only ground of reality, succeeds in keeping emotional discord out of consciousness, will cease to contribute the seeds of discord to his sub-conscious mind; and the discordant phases of the sub-conscious mind, being no longer fed, soon starve to death. As discordant sub-consciousness is thus weakened more and more, to the vanishing point, it gradually, and often very rapidly, loses its seeming power to bring forth ills in the body; and, for that reason in part, there is a more or less rapid recovery of health — which, however, is mainly due to a more positive reason, to be next discussed.

Many students of Christian Science find themselves, at the start, obliged to accept God as the working Principle, purely on the basis of revelation in the Bible and on the basis of logic, since they have little *feeling* of or for God. But, if they really trust the validity

God-Consciousness vs Sub-Consciousness

of their logic, and accept God as the only reason, and on that basis rule out discordant emotions in the manner we have described, they soon find themselves *loving* the Principle, the God, whom they prove in daily experience to be their helper in casting out the ill feelings which formerly vexed them; and, with increasing experience, this sense of love grows apace. Moreover, following this course, they soon find themselves maintaining an uninterrupted peace of mind, in a manner before unknown. As the conviction dawns upon them that, through reliance on God as the only explanation of reality, they can really hold their peace against various human temptations to discord, they find themselves experiencing a sense of power, of self-government and of joy which they had not known before. The peace, joy, and love, which come into their experience when God is thus proven to be their Helper, constitute "gold tried in the fire," and "the riches of the kingdom of heaven."

Through continuous reliance upon God, the thought and feeling of God come more and more into the forefront of consciousness, until there is scarcely a moment of the day when one does not have a sense of the divine presence. In proportion as the sub-consciousness, being starved and depleted, loses its control over the body, in the same proportion the God-consciousness is developed; and the human sense of body comes under the control of this right sense, consciousness of Truth and Love. It begins to reflect harmony instead of discord, and this process goes on until the healing is complete. A human being who has been thus freed from sub-conscious discord, and whose God-consciousness has been highly developed, is largely immune from harm by mental malpractice from others, even without much special work for protection; but those who have not attained a firm and unbroken hold upon God need more frequently to do special work against various forms of malpractice.

In this connection, it is easy to answer the question sometimes raised, as to wherein Christian Science treatment differs from mental science and suggestive therapeutics, and as to why work in

Science does not amount to the same thing as what is known as "giving suggestion to sub-consciousness." Methods of treatment by "suggestion" assume that healing can be accomplished by addressing the sub-consciousness with arguments of health and strength, made as mere statements, and not based on divine Truth. The assumption is that, in this manner, a sense of harmony can be injected into the sub-consciousness, so that it will be reflected in the body. Such an assumption is based on an expectation of filling the sub-consciousness with something that it did not previously possess. On the other hand, the Christian Science method of work tends to starve and destroy the sub-consciousness, on its discordant side, in the manner already described, and tends to build up in the person a God-consciousness, which is not *sub*-consciousness, but is, from the ordinary human standpoint, *super*-consciousness. This spiritual consciousness is humanity's birthright, which, however, can be attained only by earnest endeavor to have "that Mind which was in Christ Jesus."

How interesting and illuminating, in this connection, is Paul's statement, "If the spirit of God [God-consciousness] dwell in you, he [that same consciousness] that raised up Christ from the dead shall also quicken [make strong and well] your mortal body, by His Spirit that dwelleth in you."

God, who is immortal Mind, never created any mortal mind, whether conscious or sub-conscious. Hence, in reality there is no sub-conscious mind. Therefore it cannot be a channel for the transmission of beliefs of heredity, and it cannot be a storehouse for erroneous beliefs or a seat of evil habits. It cannot be a medium for the transmission of mortal thought, feeling or will-power. It cannot mis-govern the body. God alone governs.

Note: At the time Mrs. Eddy wrote *Science and Health*, the word *sub-consciousness* was not in common use; so she used the phrase "unconscious mortal mind" to express the same idea. For example, see *Science and Health*, 409:9-15.

GOD THE REWARDER

In the 11th chapter of Hebrews, we read: "He that cometh to God must believe that He is, and that He is a rewarder of them that diligently seek Him." This verse, rightly understood and applied, furnishes us with directions for overcoming our physical ills, as well as all other forms of evil and limitation. To make this evident, let us spend a moment in analyzing certain of the claims of error.

Contrary to the usually accepted belief, the body, as such, is incapable of experiencing either pain or pleasure. If it were, a corpse would experience pain or pleasure. It is only when consciousness is connected with the body that pain or pleasure can be experienced. This shows that, in reality, it is consciousness that aches, or burns, or smarts, or feels weak. The word *disease* means dis-ease; and it is consciousness that is dis-easy, if there is any disease, and not the body. When there is dis-ease, the body is often correspondingly abnormal, through swellings, false growths, sores, or wastings; and the discomfort seems to be located in or at these abnormal portions of the body. Consequently, it has usually been inferred that the abnormal condition of the body causes the discomfort of the mind; but exactly the reverse is true, as can be proven in two ways.

If consciousness becomes disassociated from the body through death, the swellings, false growths, sores, or wastings, may remain on the body, but they no longer occasion discomfort in any way, either to the body or to the mind, showing that flesh, as such, is incapable of sensation. Neither will abnormal conditions (except the general condition of decay) develop in the body, when consciousness is not associated with it. This shows that discord is not first in the body, and afterwards in consciousness, but is first in consciousness, and then is manifest on the body as a result.

To be sure, it must be admitted that a swelling, or sore, often develops to quite an extent on the body before the active mind discovers its appearance there or notices pain from it; and this fact has caused the vast majority of mankind to believe that disease originates in the body, and afterwards begins to disturb the mind; but the fact is, that the human mind (which is the mind that we must deal with when we are analyzing the claim of error) has a sub-conscious phase, through which the body is mostly governed, unless God's government is being scientifically demonstrated. Disease usually begins in this sub-conscious phase of the human mind, and then begins to be manifest on or in the body, and then, last of all, begins to disturb the conscious mind. In the analysis of error, falsehood, or unreality, it is the so-called sub-conscious mind, of whose operations little has been known until lately, that is the chief channel and seat of disease and sin, so far as the mortal individual is concerned. In the absence of control by divine Mind, the conscious and sub-conscious mortal mind act and react upon each other, and educate each other in sin and disease, using the body as a go-between, a mere football, as it were, to be kicked back and forth between conscious and sub-conscious arguments of evil; but the sub-conscious mind is the original sinner; and, unless prevented from doing so by the Christ-mind, it recurrently, and often continually, throws up into the conscious mind all manner of sinful and painful feelings; and the conscious mind thinks that the body is the source or cause of these sinful or painful feelings, instead of discerning the deeper source of evil in the mortal sub-consciousness. It is this mortal sub-consciousness that must be cleansed by the application of divine Mind, in order to rid both the conscious mind and the body of evil and discord. The method of doing this will be spoken of a bit later.

The second proof that abnormalities in the body are not the cause of discomfort in consciousness, is the fact that the pain or other discomfort in the mind is often completely removed hours, and sometimes weeks, before the swellings or false growths, which at one time seemed painful, have disappeared from the body. If these abnormalities of the body were the cause of mental distress, mental distress could not disappear until the physical abnormalities had been overcome. Almost invariably, the removal of discomfort from the mind through Christian Science treatment is followed, sooner or later, by normal conditions of the body.

It has now been clearly shown that all disease originates mentally, and is located in consciousness, and that abnormalities of the body are not, strictly speaking, disease, because they are not dis-ease, but are mere manifestations or effects of disease — never its cause. Hence, it is evident that the proper effort to cure disease must center its activity on removing evil from the consciousness; and if it be removed from the consciousness, it will disappear from the body automatically. That which is to be treated is the mind and not the body.

It must be entirely evident, on statement, that a dis-eased or dis-easy mind is an evil mind; and that the way to overcome an evil mind is to attack it with that which is opposed to it, namely, good Mind. Now there is only good Mind. Christ Jesus declared: "There is none good, save one; that is God." If we *intelligently and persistently* turn to this good Mind, God, that Mind will remove evil from our consciousness as naturally as the sun removes darkness from our eyes, when we turn from darkness toward the sun.

Whoever beholds the light of the sun, beholds coincidentally rays of violet, indigo, blue, green, yellow, orange, red, and every intermediary shade and tint of color, all beautifully blended together in what we call light. Likewise, whoever *diligently* turns to God, and mentally beholds Him, cannot fail to increasingly behold, and to gradually receive into his own consciousness, love, joy, peace, strength, harmony, health, substance, plenty, entertainment, intelligence, and life, all beautifully blended together in that "true light, which lighteth every man that cometh into the world;" for God is omnipresent, not beyond the reach of any man's mental gaze; yea,

He is in every man's very heart, when that man will diligently open his heart to God.

So if we turn to God, knowing that He is here, and if we diligently seek Him, He will reward us by shining in our hearts and minds with every conceivable form of good; and in proportion as this comes to pass, in that proportion the darkness of sin and disease are driven from every phase of the human consciousness, and we are healed, or made whole, in consciousness — just where we need to be healed; and then the body soon automatically reflects the divine harmony which, through the power of God, has been established in the mind. Accordingly, in the treatment of disease, the advice of Paul is most excellent: "Be willing [be choosing] to be absent from the body [in thought], and present with the Lord." For God is the healer; and He will reward us with healing, if we come to Him with diligence.

* * * * * * *

Suppose darkness should say to itself, "I am going to rise up and attack light." What would become of the darkness when it got within reaching distance of the light? How much would it accomplish aside from its own destruction? *Moral*: If there be no error (darkness) in a man's own consciousness, the errors of his ancestors, and all adverse thought-influences, will be as powerless to harm him as darkness is powerless to harm light. And this is true by gradation as well as true as a matter of complete attainment. The elimination of any portion or kind of error from a man's own consciousness, through turning to God, renders him more immune from the attacks of any form of error originating from without.

THE MARRIAGE OF TRUTH AND LOVE

In the divine Mind, truth and love are constantly and indissolubly wedded. All human undertakings which are to count for anything must exemplify this union, for it is "according to the pattern shewed to thee in the mount." "Be ye perfect, even as your Father which is in heaven is perfect."

It is one of the "wiles of the devil" to try to divorce truth and love in the consciousness of men, and to make them believe that truth can be advanced through war and strife, carried on with motives of anger, hatred, revenge, self-interest, or self-justification. Ever and anon, problems of importance must be discussed and settled in our families, in our churches, in our business relations, and in the larger negotiations of politics, law, government, religion, and diplomacy. In these discussions, let us defeat the "one evil" through understanding and bearing in mind that, by no amount of argument, however valid, and by no amount of force of any kind, can we successfully promulgate truth and permanently bring to pass the correct issue, unless, during our efforts, we purposely and habitually exercise the spirit of good-will. In dealing with others, reasoning and good-will are as the wings of a bird. If a bird tries to fly with only one wing, he whirls round and round, to his own confusion, getting nowhere; but using both wings, he makes much progress.

Only as the male principle, truth, and the female principle, love, are wedded in our consciousness, can we obey the spiritual command: "Be fruitful [of righteous thoughts and deeds], and multiply [them], and replenish the earth [with them], and subdue it." Truth will go no farther and no faster than love goes as a companion. "What therefore God hath joined together, let not man put asunder."

Dominion Within

Toil on, then, thou art in the right,
However narrow souls may call thee wrong.
Be as thou wouldst be in thine own clear sight,
And so thou shalt be in the world's ere long.
                                   Lowell

"LET YOUR CONVERSATION BE IN HEAVEN"

Experience and conversation have led the writer to believe that there are many students of Christian Science, who have a correct theoretical understanding of its fundamental doctrines, when they attempt to apply Science in the treatment of themselves or others, fall into the error of holding the material body, or some of its parts or organs, in thought, while making their declarations of divine harmony, health, strength and perfection. In doing so, they unwittingly fall into the fundamental error of practically declaring that there is a material man, when Principle demands that declarations of harmony and perfection be made only with regard to the real man, who is spiritual and perfect, like unto his Father. To make declarations of harmony and perfection about the projections of false material sense is foolish; it is but a phase of mesmerism.

Other students of Christian Science sometimes fall into a yet more subtle error, especially while treating themselves. They correctly make their declarations of the harmony and perfection of the real, spiritual man; but while doing so, they are watching the body "out of the corners of their eyes," so to speak, to see whether the treatment is taking effect, thus implicitly admitting that there is a material, as well as a spiritual man. This procedure does not constitute that undivided affirmation of Truth, and that absolute separation from error, from the false concept of man, which yields genuine and permanent results. There is in Science no material body to be healed. What appears as such, is simply one of the phases of false belief. False sense is that which is to be healed by being destroyed. There is nothing else to be taken account of.

To be sure, the body seems to be uttering complaints, else no treatment would be undertaken; but these complaints are to be recognized as complaints of false material sense, of which the body itself is a part. Many times, these complaints do not at once disappear under treatment, and so, for a time, cannot fully be eliminated from our human consciousness; and many do not seem to find the scientific way to deal with them.

To illustrate this, suppose one were carrying on an important business conversation with a caller in a room where there was an assertive and talkative child. He would doubtless endeavor to quiet the child, if he could not put him out of the room; but, if, for the time being, he could not induce him to be still, he would go on with his conversation, concentrating his attention upon the subject in hand, which he could do if he chose, regardless of the child's babbling. He would, in a way, be conscious of the noise, but he would not allow it to interrupt the train of his thought. If the child became too assertive, he might pause momentarily now and then to command it to be still, and thus lessen the uproar in a measure; but, if he paid no attention to the child's racket, it would in all probability grow quiet all the more speedily.

In treatment, it is our endeavor to hold conversation with our highest sense of good and truth, to enter into communion with Truth and Love, to hold converse with God. In doing this, we obey the injunction: "Let your conversation be in heaven" — that is, our conversation is in and with Truth, in and with harmonious consciousness, which is heaven. In this conversation, the sense of matter and discord can have no rightful place. To the degree that we admit the thought of matter, even to watch its supposed states, to that degree our conversation ceases to be in heaven, for we have admitted the thought of a lie. If the sense of body and discord becomes too assertive, we may pause now and then to quiet this false sense by denying that there is any material body, or any discord. Indeed, we may meet any specific claim of discord by a specific form of denial adapted thereto; but we should never be betrayed into affirming harmony with regard to the physical body, or into watching for harmony to be manifest in the physical body, with the thought or implicit belief that the body is real. Many times, it is most efficacious to frame a line of thought in truth, including affirmations calculated to specifically offset the false claims which the body seems to be uttering, and then to fix our attention upon the affirmation of these declarations of truth, and hold to them, until, without narrowly watching the process, we become aware that the body has ceased to utter its complaints. The old proverb finds good application here: "The watched pot never boils." To fix our attention upon declarations of truth is to heal by spiritual realization. To deny the existence of the material body, and of pain, weakness, discord, is to heal by argument. The two methods may be resorted to successively; but affirmation of truth should never be made concerning the material body, and, of course, denials are never called for in connection with things spiritual.

  The multiplication table is a compound idea, of which the ideas expressed by the words "four times three equals twelve," "five times six equals thirty," etc., are simple ideas. These simple ideas can be used individually, yet they cannot for an instant be so separated from the multiplication table so that the multiplication table does not contain them. So the multiplication table, although compound, is nevertheless indivisible, since no component part can be for an instant separated from it. Therefore the multiplication table is individual, since "individual" and "indivisible" are synonymous terms as used in philosophy. So also, as Mrs. Eddy teaches, man is the compound yet individual idea of God (*Science and Health* 468:22; 475:14) The functions and activities of the real man are simpler ideas which go to make up that compound idea, which man is; but no one of these simpler ideas can for an instant be separated from the compound idea; hence the compound idea is individual.

  Man reflects God, who is omnipresent Life, infinite Mind — all-powerful, all-harmonious and eternally active. Hence, in his every function and activity, man may be declared to be an idea of God, from which life and strength and harmony are never for an instant separated. To hold in thought such declarations as these, and many others which are given in the Bible, in our textbook, and in other Christian Science literature, is to have our "conversation in heaven." It is well to keep our conversation in heaven, and to keep it from dropping to the earth of material sense as much as possible. To keep our conversation in heaven is to "pray without ceasing," to "meditate in the law of the Lord," and to "seek the kingdom of God and His righteousness." If we do this, all needed harmony will be "added" to our human sense, without our "taking thought" for materiality, until such time as material sense shall have been entirely eliminated. "Let your conversation be in heaven."

* * * * * * *

If there is nothing within which can be "hurt," nothing without can hurt us. Darkness cannot harm light, and mortal mind cannot harm the divine Mind or its reflection; it cannot even touch it. Therefore, if we reflect the divine Mind, we shall not be "hurt" by the injustice, or coldness, or misjudgment of others, no matter how much, from a mortal standpoint, we should be justified in feeling so. One finds by experience that he cannot *afford* to let himself be stirred up by what others do or do not do, by what they say or do not say. One should let all these things slip off, "like water off a duck's back." It behooves us to be so much unselfed, so freed from everything that is unlike the divine Mind, that there is nothing within to be disturbed by the manifestations of error.

"PERFECT LOVE CASTETH OUT FEAR"

To many students of the Scriptures, this text does not seem perfectly clear; for they are unable to see just how love can be a special antidote for fear. It would seem that faith is the more direct opposite. Then, also, the question arises, How is perfect love to be attained?

A solution to these difficulties appears, if the order of the words in the text is inverted, so that it reads, *Love of the perfect casteth out fear.* Perfect love must necessarily be love of the perfect; for love of the imperfect could not be perfect love. Accordingly, to attain perfect love, we must learn, and in Christian Science we can learn, what the perfect is, and then we shall learn to love the perfect.

What is the occasion of fear? It arises when we anticipate the prospective or continued loss of something or someone that we love. We think that we are, or are going to be, deprived of health, strength, property (substance), life, or the presence or life of some person whom we love. But, in Christian Science, we learn that the only real health is divine harmony, which is the eternal, indestructible, changeless, omnipresent law of God; and we learn that the only real strength is God's omnipresent and indestructible power; and that the only real property (substance) is Spirit, infinite Mind and its ideas; that life is God or the expression of God, and is omnipresent. These real entities are the perfect entities, and no others are perfect or real. If, therefore, we have learned to love these, and have withdrawn our love from their false, material counterfeits, our love has become perfect, and is fixed upon objects or entities which we know we cannot lose or be separated from, since they are omnipresent and eternal. Therefore, when our love has become perfect through love of the perfect, we know that we cannot lose anything that we love, and so we have no occasion for fear. Therefore, "perfect love casteth out fear." It is also manifest that, "He that feareth is not made perfect in love"' for he has not learned to love the perfect, and the perfect only.

    A child and his mother are walking in the field. The child stops to gather some buttercups; the mother strolls on. Suddenly the child looks up and sees his mother quite a distance away. In a paroxysm of fear, he cries: "Mama! Mama! wait for me!" If the mother stops, his fear promptly subsides, and he does not specially mind toddling along over the intervening distance, until he catches up with her. When we are afraid, it is mostly because we think that life, or something or somebody that we love is getting away from us; but when, through Science, we become really convinced that Life and all good things will wait until we catch up — until we attain the realization of them, most of our fear subsides; and we do not so much mind the period of struggle that must be gone through before we gain the permanent possession of the good we seek.

    In this connection is seen the great wisdom of Paul's exhortation, "Set your affections on things above, not on things on the earth." In proportion as we obey this injunction, we are freed from any occasion for fear, anxiety, foreboding, or doubt, and we enter more and more into love, joy, peace, and the realization of all good.

* * * * * * *

    Discouragement is the more sinister because it is generally looked upon as harmless. In fable it is told that the devil one night held a sale and offered all his tools to anyone who would pay his price. These were spread out for sale, some labeled hatred, and envy, and sickness, and sensuality, and despair, and crime — a motley array. Apart from the rest lay a harmless-looking, wedge-shaped implement marked "discouragement." It was much worn and was priced above the rest, showing that it was held in high esteem by its owner. When asked the reason the devil replied,

"Perfect Love Casteth out Fear"

"I can use this more easily than any of the others, for so few know it belongs to me. With this I can open doors that I can not budge with the others, and once I get inside I can use which ever of them suits me best."
William R. Rathvon
The Christian Science Journal, May 1911.

WORKING OUT OUR PROBLEM
(From the *Christian Science Sentinel*, November 14, 1908)

Many students of Christian Science, as well as Christian people generally, make a mistake in attempting too much at the start, or rather in not rightly selecting the phase or manifestation of error over which they attempt to demonstrate at the beginning. Error as a whole presents many problems to be solved, and no young student of Christianity is competent to work on them all at the same time, and find success in his efforts. He must choose among the problems, working them one at a time, although it is true that the solving of any one problem contributes to the solution of all the rest.

The most frequent mistakes made by many who are trying to be Christian Scientists is in attempting to demonstrate peace without, before they have demonstrated peace within. They think they must solve the world's problems, or their church's problems, or at least the problems of their family or friends, in order to solve their own. The scientific order of demonstration is the exact reverse. A man must cast the beam out of his own eye before he can see clearly to cast the mote out of his brother's eye. We must be sufficiently acquainted with God, good, and sufficiently grounded in our consciousness of Him, sufficiently able to dwell "in the secret place of the most High," so that in our own consciousness we have become largely impervious to the darts of error, before we are strongly enough placed in good to be of very much service to other people. If we have not a firm inward hold on peace and harmony, we shall not do much toward imparting these qualities to other people or to outward situations.

Beginners in Christian Science need to follow the example of Jesus. Before he entered upon his ministry, he went apart, for forty days, into the wilderness, to pray. He saw that each should have his own consciousness closely and firmly and unalterably united with God, good, before undertaking the problems of the world. During these forty days, there were sick to be healed, there were evils to be cast out, there were wrongs to be righted; but for the time Jesus paid no attention to them; he was giving his entire attention to getting so firmly placed and grounded in the abiding consciousness of God, good, that he would be able to attack these evils all the more successfully later on, and without being himself overthrown in the process.

We do not need to make a physical journey into a material desert in order to follow the example given us by Jesus in this particular. It is sufficient to withdraw our thoughts from other people's problems for a time, so that we may give our entire attention to the solution of our own — become sufficiently acquainted with God so that we shall be permanently at peace within, even while the storms of error rage all around us. When we have demonstrated such inward and abiding peace that feelings of anger, jealousy, envy, resentment, self-pity, brooding over wrongs, and the like, are not stirred into activity by the conduct of others, then we have gotten into a position to be of real service in overcoming the errors in our family, in the church, and in the world at large. Of course, such a demonstration is a matter of degree. Probably there are very few who have reached such a height of spiritual attainment that inharmonious feelings are not at times aroused into momentary activity; but we must have become sufficiently assimilated to God, sufficiently habituated in the abiding consciousness of good, sufficiently alert with regard to error, so that we promptly put out these intruders upon harmonious consciousness, instead of admitting and cherishing them, before we can be very helpful to others.

Even in the experience of those strongest in the truth, there come times when, to sense, error specially abounds and rages. In such a time, a Christian's first duty is to save his own sense from taking part in the raging of error. With his utmost efforts this may be all he is able to do, and he will do well at times, if he does this; but, unless he does this first of all, he can neither help himself nor anyone else. Such a raging of error is spoken of by the prophet Ezekiel, and he tells us: "Though these three men, Noah, Daniel, and Job, were in it, they should deliver but their own souls by their righteousness, said the Lord God." If these mighty men of faith, under the given unfavorable conditions, would have been able to have saved but their own sense from having part in error, able to have done no more than maintain spiritual consciousness, then surely there are times when we, who have not endured the test of the flood, nor the trial by suffering and the loss of all earthly possessions, and who have not survived the lions' den — there are times when we shall do well if we do nothing more than maintain our own peace.

In this connection, the story of Noah and the ark is illuminating. Taken figuratively, the flood may represent the raging sea of error; the solid ground the abiding sense of good, which for a time seemed to be completely covered and hidden from sight by the sea; while the ark represents that spiritual consciousness which rides safely above the raging waves. Spiritual consciousness was a place of safety to Noah, his sons, and their wives; but there were none others in the world who were able to dwell in this ark of spiritual consciousness; and so no other men were saved from the flood. The ark had but one window, and it was open toward heaven, toward light and truth and good — the ark had no windows at the sides for looking out on the sea of error. From time to time, Noah sent out a thought of peace, the dove; but it found no resting place, none of the solid ground of good appearing above the flood; and so it returned to Noah. Thus he knew that the waters of error were not yet subsided, and he continued to dwell in the ark of spiritual consciousness until error should destroy itself, and thus abate, at least in some measure. When once more Noah sent out the dove, his thought of peace, it found a resting place, and did not return. Then he knew that error was sufficiently self-destroyed, and enough of truth and good had appeared in the outward situation so that it was safe for him to begin to make preparations to go forth from the ark — that is, to reach out with aspiring faith for the benefit of mankind.

Many times there are members of our family, or of our church, or people in our neighborhood, who are so satisfied with their present condition that the wisest thing we can do is to protect our own consciousness and allow the error to find its own self-destruction, while we calmly abide in the consciousness that nothing real, nothing good, can be destroyed or lost.

When error has sufficiently destroyed itself in the consciousness of others through suffering, the time will come when they will be ready for the help which we can give them. It is well for us occasionally to utter a word of peace, a thought of Science; but if their behavior does not indicate that this thought of Science finds a place in their consciousness where it can rest without stirring up violent manifestations of error, the thing for us to do is to continue to dwell quietly in the ark of our consciousness of Truth. If, in our efforts to help them, we ourselves are dragged forth from the ark into the sea of error, much is lost to us and to them. While the prodigal chose to remain in the far country, "no man ministered unto him." By these words, Jesus seems to intimate quite clearly that to let them alone is the most effective treatment for those who are headstrong in error.

The proper interpretation of certain verses in the first chapter of Genesis gives us added understanding of our privilege and duty. God's universe was never "created" in the sense of having been developed from a previous state of non-existence. God's universe is co-eternal with Himself. Any well-instructed Christian Scientist will recognize this fact, without argument from the Scripture to support it, though such evidence can readily be given. The record in the first chapter of Genesis is not, therefore, a record of creation, but a record of the inspired writer's advancing periods of understanding of the universe which eternally existed. Says Mrs. Eddy in *Science and Health*, "Was not this a revelation instead of a creation? The successive appearing of God's ideas is represented as taking place on so many *evenings* and *mornings* — words which indicate, in the absence of solar time, spiritually clearer views of Him, views which are not implied by material darkness and dawn."

While we are passing through the advancing periods of understanding, the human sense may be subject to more or less of disquietude and unrest. There will be "days" when all will appear bright and clear. Then other problems will arise, which we are not able to solve for a time, and we may pass through a period of "night." Then we succeed in solving or overcoming these difficulties of understanding or experience, and come into a brighter and fuller "day." Finally, we arrive at the goal of complete understanding, where we know the truth, and know that we know it, and feel scientifically confident that we can abide in the consciousness of Truth and protect ourselves from coming under the domination of error. While there is much that we have not demonstrated, yet we feel that we understand God, understand His universe, and understand ourselves, and that we have sufficient hold on the truth, so that we can make our way forward gradually to a complete demonstration of that which we know to be true, without let or hindrance from error.

When we have attained this consciousness, we have reached the day of rest — not a period of idleness, by any means, but rather a period of activity in demonstration of the truth. Like God, we are able to "rest in action." (*Science and Health*) We work vigorously for our own advancement and the advancement of others. While doing so, we are confronted with all sorts of errors, but they do not disturb the harmony of our consciousness while we are overcoming them. We are strong enough in the truth so that they cannot disturb us. So we are in perfect repose, even while we are actively working. This period of repose, this day of rest, is our Sabbath day. We should "remember the Sabbath day, to keep it holy;" that is, our consciousness should rest in God, and we should not allow inharmonious, annoying, unholy thoughts and feelings to enter. We should keep our consciousness pure and clear and our Sabbath day, our spiritual consciousness, having been attained, should endure forever.

* * * * * * *

Despite the prosperity of my church, it was learned that material organization has its value and peril, and that organization is requisite only in the earliest periods in Christian history. After this material form of cohesion and fellowship has accomplished its end, continued organization retards spiritual growth, and should be laid off — even as the corporeal organization deemed requisite in the first stages of mortal existence is finally laid off, in order to gain spiritual freedom and supremacy. . . Material organization wars with Love's spiritual compact.

Mary Baker Eddy
Retrospection and Introspection

THE URGE OF GOD

In the original Greek of the New Testament occurs several places the phrase *orge theou* pronounced or-gay the-ou, which most of the translators render, "the wrath of God." For instance, in Romans 1:18 we read: "For the wrath of God is revealed from heaven against all ungodliness, and unrighteousness of men." This translation almost wholly misrepresents the true meaning of the Greek phrase, as we shall see.

Nearly all the peoples of ancient and modern Europe were and are descended from an ancient people named the "Aryans," who originally inhabited the table-land of central Asia, but made their way westward into Europe in several successive migrations. The languages spoken by most of the peoples of ancient and modern Europe represent modifications of the language of the ancient Aryans. The vast majority of the changes and modifications which make the different European languages so diverse from each other, took place before the art of writing was invented or was in common use, and before there was much intercommunication among tribes and nations through travel.

One of the migrations from the table-land of Asia went westward into Southern Europe, and finally separated. A portion went southward into what is now known as the Grecian peninsula, and became the progenitors of the ancient Greek nation. Another portion went into what is now known as the Italian peninsula, and became the progenitors of the ancient Latin and other tribes, which finally united to make the Roman nation.

Before this separation took place, there was a verb in use, which, when the art of writing was developed among the Greeks, came to be pronounced and spelled *orgao,* but among the Romans, came to be pronounced and spelled *urgeo.* From this Greek verb was formed the noun *orge,* and another noun *orgia*, from what is derived our English word *orgy*. From the Latin verb is derived our English *urge*. Allied to these in derivation, though not quite so directly or evidently, is the English word *work*, which came through the Saxon language, derived from the ancient Aryan.

We are able to form a very correct idea of the significance of *orge* from these words, *orgy*, *urge* and *work*, allied to it by derivation. The primary sense of *orgy* is unbridled, unlimited, unrestrained action. The sense of the other two words is sufficiently evident. Liddell and Scott's Greek lexicon gives as the primary meaning of *orge* "natural impulse," and gives as other meanings, "disposition, nature, heart."

Accordingly, it should be easy to discern that the correct sense of the Greek phrase *orge theou* is given by such expressions as, "the natural impulse of good or Love," "the work of good," "the unbridled or unlimited action of divine Love." Neither in this phrase, nor in any other phrase in the New Testament, when correctly translated, is there any suggestion of anything akin to human wrath or anger manifested by God. The sense of *orge theou* is that of divine Love overcoming evil with good. The correct rendering of the verse quoted from Romans would be: The nature (urgency, unrestrained power) of God is revealed from heaven against all ungodliness and unrighteousness of men. (Rom. 1:18)

The correct sense of this Greek phrase is of great use in Christian Science treatment, since it enables us to realize something of the constant impulsion, the unrestrained nature, the riotous profusion of the power of good, of the power of love, joy, harmony, substance, which are *a law of annihilation* to all beliefs or manifestations of hatred, malice, jealousy, grief, discord, poverty, inertia, stagnation, or death.

In the 19th Psalm, the sun is poetically described " . . . as a bridegroom coming out of his chamber, and rejoiceth as a strong man to run a race. His going forth is from the end of heaven, and his circuit unto the ends of the it: and there is nothing hid from the heat thereof." The sun constantly irradiates light and heat — not for the purpose of dispelling darkness or cold, but because it is *the nature* of the sun to constantly send forth light and heat with tremendous energy. If darkness or cold get in the sun's way, they are destroyed. Likewise, it is *the nature* of God to constantly irradiate with tremendous energy into the whole realm of being life, strength, harmony, plenty, love and joy. If beliefs of stagnation, death, weakness, disease, hatred, malice, poverty, or grief, seem to get in God's way, the *orgy*, the unbridled action of God destroys them; and, if we realize this, these beliefs will be destroyed for us.

* * * * * * *

When students have fulfilled all the good ends of organization, and are convinced that by leaving the material forms thereof a higher spiritual unity is won, then is the time to follow the example of the *Alma Mater*. Material organization is requisite in the beginning, but when it has done its work, the purely Christly method of teaching and preaching must be adopted. . . The real Christian compact is love for one another. This bond is wholly spiritual and inviolate.

Mary Baker Eddy
Miscellaneous Writings

WORK FOR THE PATIENT
(From a Letter to a Patient)

There are certain things that you should have in mind and work for in your reading. In the first place, you should find reasons for understanding, in theory, that there is no matter, hence no life, intelligence, sensation, strength, or substance in matter. You will not be able for years or perhaps for centuries to come, to overcome and lose all sense of matter; yet you should find reasons for understanding that there actually is no matter. In *Science and Health*, we read; "The verity of Mind shows conclusively how it is that matter seems to be, but is not."

In school, you found reasons for understanding that the sun does not rise, but that it stands still while the earth revolves; but you have not yet been able to make this evident to your eyes. You can find reasons for knowing that the rails on a straight, level railroad track do not run together at a point on the horizon, yet you cannot make this evident to your eyes. In like manner, you can find reasons for understanding that there is no life, truth, intelligence, substance, health, strength, or sensation in matter, even though you cannot at present prevent your physical senses from testifying to the contrary. You *will* be able to make the truth evident *in part*. You *will* soon be able to prove to yourself that there is far less sensation in matter than you at present feel. You *will* soon be able to prove *largely* that strength and health are not from matter *but from Mind, God. And it is important that you find this out.*

If an engineer trusted his eyes, because of the rails seeming to converge he would not dare to go ahead with his train, lest it should run off the track; but, trusting his reason instead of his eyes, he goes ahead. So if you use your reason, taking God as the premise for your reasoning instead of trusting the false evidence of your physical senses, you will go ahead and get well, even though the senses are trying to tell you that you will continue to be ill, or that you are going to run into the ditch for a smash-up.

You should find reasons for understanding that life, truth, intelligence, health, strength and all good things are from God, infinite Mind, and that these things are really eternal and indestructible. To a very large degree, you can gain the realization of these facts here and now — to a degree large enough so that you will be stronger and healthier than ever before in your life, and so that you will live more years on the earth than you would have lived without this knowledge of the Science of Christianity, even if you had not had your present sickness.

Also, from your reading, you should find reasons for understanding that in reality there is no sin and no sickness, and that there never was any, because the infinite God, who is wholly good and who created all, never made any. Sin and sickness are delusions of the human consciousness — not states of the body — delusions which by the knowledge of the Truth, as above described, can and will be cast out. Jesus said, "Ye shall know the Truth and the Truth shall make you free." Through the knowledge of the Truth, you will be able to prove, here and now in your person, the nothingness of sin and sickness; for, if they were *something*, God Himself could not destroy them; but being illusions, mistaken beliefs (though seeming very real), they can be destroyed.

Also, from your reading, you should find reasons for understanding what Jesus meant when he said: "Call no man your father upon the earth; for One is your Father, even God." You should learn to understand that the human sense of life and generation is a false sense; that, in reality, your only true parentage is in God, and hence your only heritage is good. In truth, there is no mortal law of heredity. "What mean ye, that ye use this proverb, saying, The fathers have eaten sour grapes and the children's teeth are set on edge? As I live, saith the Lord God, ye shall not have occasion to use this proverb. Behold, all souls are Mine; as the soul of the father, so also the soul of the son, is Mine, saith the Lord God." Since God is the only creator, man is not a creator. Hence, God alone is Father-Mother, and man is not a father and woman is not a mother (See Matt. 13:47-50). God is "our Father which art in heaven," and there is in reality no parent beside Him. When we find this out and make it real to ourselves, we shall find ourselves inheriting good only. There is nothing in this teaching to interfere with the fullest degree of love toward those whom we call parents. We are no longer to regard them as parents in a fundamental sense; but we are to love them because they are children of God, brothers and sisters in the Lord. (See Matt. 12:47-50)

You should learn to understand that your life is eternally "hid with Christ in God," and that nothing can attack or destroy your life; that the false sense of sin, disease, and death *cannot even seem to attack it, as soon as you know enough of Truth to cast false sense out.* Christ said: "If a man keep my saying, he shall never see death," and it is possible for you to learn, understand, and keep his saying, and thus not see death — at least for years and years to come. If you could understand and keep his saying wholly, you would never see death at all. Perhaps you cannot do this wholly; but you can do it sufficiently for all present purposes; for thousands, who were worse off than you are, have done so before you in the last forty years.

You should study your textbook, *Science and Health*, and such other literature as your practitioner directs, faithfully according to your strength, and try to find reasons for understanding the things above outlined; and you should *not worry* if the understanding does not come very rapidly; it will come in due time. Do just as you used to do in school. You tried each day to understand the books which you were studying, and you gained a little more knowledge each day, and you were reasonably content. You were not surprised nor discouraged, and you did not worry, because you did not understand the whole book, or even everything in the day's lesson, during the first few weeks that you studied the book. You felt confident that you would learn all about it in time, and so you were satisfied with each day's attainment. In like manner, study *Science and Health* and the other literature. Study with confidence and diligence, yet without a sense of haste; and the understanding will gradually come; and as the understanding comes, the healing will come. Meanwhile, the mental work that your practitioner does for you, the understanding of these truths that he holds for you, will be of great assistance to you, and may heal you before you come to the understanding for yourself. But there is no danger of your learning too much or too rapidly.

You would do well to commit to memory as soon as convenient the following verses of Scripture: Isa.40:31; Gal. 5:16; Rom.6:12; Gal.5:24,25; II Tim.1:7.

Also commit to memory as soon as possible the following passages from *Science and Health*: Page 76:22-25; page 326:16-21; page 327:1-7, page 468:7-15. Read two or three times per week page 390, line 12 to page 393, line 21.

* * * * * * *

Such books as will rule disease out of mortal mind — and so efface the images and thoughts of disease, instead of impressing them with forcible descriptions of medical details, will help to abate sickness and to destroy it.

Mary Baker Eddy
Science and Health

SELF-SURRENDER THROUGH LOVE

A person who is seeking healing, or the solution of any other specific problem, through Christian Science, is scarcely forgetting self while working on that problem directly, no matter how correct the metaphysical declarations and the denials of error which he is making. Such a line of work is legitimate, but it is an open question whether it is always the most effective. In military activities, many a position of an enemy can be carried by a flank movement that could not be carried by a direct attack, and this fact illustrates what is often true in the Christian life. In the matter of good food and clothing, Jesus told us not to seek them directly, but to seek first the kingdom of God and his righteousness, and let them be added. The same general procedures also are frequently an excellent one for overcoming sickness and sin. If we can effectively seek and gain the kingdom of God in a general way — in ways that have no direct bearing upon our specific personal problems — we may find that, in such an hour as we think not, health and holiness along the particular lines in which we have been striving for them are added unto us. The great law of the Christian life is not so much to seek something for ourselves — however high and worthy that object may be — but to seek to forget self in the love of God and man. Some definite suggestions as to methods of doing this may be worth considering.

Any line of procedure which tends to an habitual thought and love of God and to the general spiritualization of consciousness, is exceedingly useful. One method which many follow is to set aside times and seasons in which the effort is made to withdraw thought as fully as possible from all the affairs of worldly living, and to fix it upon the facts and laws of Spirit and of the spiritual life. This is what is meant by going into one's closet to pray and by going into the desert to pray. Unquestionably such times and seasons are indispensable to the attainment of spiritual life.

But there is another method which seems to be overlooked by many. That is the method of seeing in all the affairs of normal human living a symbolic presentation of higher realities. There never can be a counterfeit along any line unless there is a genuine to be counterfeited. Christian Scientists are aware that all activities on the material plane of living are counterfeits, more or less reversed, of spiritual activities. Spirit is the real substance, and matter is the counterfeit sense of substance. God's infinite idea is the real man, and human corporealities are counterfeit presentations of man. If the real man were not feeding upon the truth and love manifested by God, the counterfeit presentations of corporeal men feeding upon material food could not appear. Unless the divine idea were ever in Mind, being thus clothed and sheltered in Mind, or Spirit, which is the true substance, the counterfeit presentations of men being clothed and housed materially could not appear. Unless the real man were being entertained by the continued contemplation of good, beauty, and harmony in infinite variety, the counterfeit presentations of corporeal men being entertained by activities of various kinds on a material basis could not appear.

On the human plane, in our present stage of advancement, we need material food, clothing, shelter and entertainment, so much so that Jesus, speaking from the human point of view, declared: "Your heavenly Father knoweth that ye have need of these things," — a statement which is not true in absolute metaphysics. The fact to be now considered and borne in mind is, that unless God were good and constantly supplying good to the real man, it would be impossible that there should be presented to us those manifestations which appear to us as good on the material plane. From this viewpoint, we are privileged to see, and to meditate upon, and to be grateful for, the goodness of God in connection with our daily eating, and being clothed and housed, and in connection with our innocent pleasures, even though they be more or less of a material order.

Self-Surrender through Love

In *Miscellaneous Writings*, Mrs. Eddy has most clearly expressed the relation which should exist between our sense of the beauties and bounties of the human world and the spiritual realities. She writes as follows: "My sense of the beauty of the universe is that beauty typifies holiness and is something to be desired. Earth is more spiritually beautiful to my gaze now than when it was more earthly to the eyes of Eve. The pleasant sensations of human belief of form and color, must be spiritualized, until we gain the glorified sense of substance as in the new heaven and earth, the harmony of body and Mind. Even the human conception of beauty, grandeur, and utility, is something that defies a sneer. It is more than imagination. It is next to divine beauty and the grandeur of Spirit. It lives with our earth-life, and is the subjective state of high thoughts."

To eat material food merely as material food with no thought of anything else, is to be carnally minded, and to act in the order of death; but to see in material eating a symbol of feeding on the body and blood of Christ — that is, of assimilating truth and love — is to be more spiritually minded and to act in the order of life. To dwell in one's earthly home, seeing in it nothing but a manifestation of matter, is to dwell in a house which is dead; but to think of the material home as a symbol of the Father's house, — "the house not made with hands, eternal in the heavens," — is to make one's thought of home filled with life. Human activities of all kinds, carried on and thought of solely on a material basis, must of necessity become dull and uninteresting; but normal human activities regarded as symbols of spiritual activities, and with the thought resting largely on the spiritual, even while the material is being performed, are filled with interest and loving gratitude to God. To see material objects and activities merely as material, is to see them as dead; but to see them as representing on the human plane spiritual ideas and activities, is to see the normal affairs of daily existence as full of life and love.

A watch which one purchases for himself may be merely a useful material article; but a watch given to one by his father or mother may be not only a useful article, but almost a constant reminder of love and providence. In the one case, one's thought of the watch is dead; in the other case, it is alive, giving much more satisfaction than in the former case. Likewise, as already suggested, it is our privilege to see in every material possession, legitimately gained and held, a symbol of our heavenly Father's love and care, thus keeping our thought constantly alive with an intelligence, perception and love of God in connection with every phase of our human living.

When a gift is given to some people, they will go through the form of thanking the donor with more or less of realized thankfulness at the time of receiving it, but will go on using this gift week after week, and year after year, without again thinking of the donor. Other people, receiving a useful gift, will frequently think of the donor when using it, and may even express their appreciation to the giver at different times. Those who soon forget the giver get far less satisfaction from the gift than do those who not only use the gift, but often think of the giver. The thought of the former class is filled with intelligence with regard to the gift which they have, while the latter class manifests non-intelligence — that is, death.

When one first begins to read a well written and newsy letter from a friend, one's attention may, at first, be somewhat directed to the paper and the character of the handwriting, but soon the attention is caught by the lines of thought which the written words symbolize; and thereafter, the attention is carried along on a plane distinctly higher than that of letter paper and written words, though the attention is directed and guided by those written characters. However, if the reader were to fix his thoughts upon the quality of the paper and the character and details of the handwriting as he went along, he would largely miss the line of thought which the written words were intended to convey. Thus he would lose the higher and more satisfying interest through a lower line of thought and love of the writer, but they symbolize and serve to convey the thought and love to one who reads the letter aright.

Material food, drink, clothing, houses, fields, landscapes, and other material objects which contribute to human comfort and satisfaction, are not creations of God; nevertheless, they may and should symbolize to human sense the intelligent care and love of God, the infinite Father. He whose thought and attention are centered on these material objects, instead of being carried above them, though in considerable degree directed and guided by them, makes the same kind of a mistake as does the reader of a letter whose thought is so much centered on the paper and the character of the handwriting that he misses the love and intelligence which the letter was intended to convey. Paul has well suggested in his letter to the Romans: "The invisible things of Him from the creation of the world are clearly seen, being understood by the things that are made, even His eternal power and Godhead."

As previously suggested, one may spiritualize his thought by withdrawing as fully as possible from all material objects and pursuits, but to spiritualize his thought by that method, he must give his entire time and attention to the effort so long as he is engaged in it. On the other hand, by cultivating the habit of seeing in material objects and pursuits symbols of higher realities and activities as between God and the spiritual man, and thus having the thought directed to spiritual things by all the details of daily living, one may have his consciousness filled with the recognition and love of God practically all of the time, even when about his normal and proper human business and recreation.

These thoughts are in distinct accord with Mrs. Eddy's teaching in *Miscellaneous Writings*, as previously quoted, and in the following paragraph: "To take all earth's beauty into one gulp of vacuity and label beauty nothing, is ignorantly to caricature God's creation, which is unjust to human sense, and to the divine realism. In our immature sense of spiritual things, let us say of the beauties of the sensuous universe: 'I love your promise; and shall know, sometime, the spiritual reality and substance of form, light, and color, of what I now through you discern dimly; and knowing this, I shall be satisfied. Matter is a frail conception of mortal mind, and mortal mind is a poorer representative of the beauty, grandeur, and glory of the immortal Mind." How truly Paul has written: "If that which was done away is glorious, how much more than which remaineth is glorious."

It is undoubtedly wise and necessary for every seeker after spiritual life to have seasons of withdrawing his thought as completely as possible from material objects and activities in order to be "alone with God," but let not this be the only reliance for spiritualizing consciousness, since very few people are so situated that they can spend any considerable portion of the day in the "closet" communion with God. In addition to this, through taking material objects and pursuits, not as finalities of thought, but as symbols of higher lines of mental activity, let the consciousness be spiritualized in every minute and hour of the day, whether in "the hour of prayer," or in the market-place, or the field, or the home, or the place of legitimate amusement.

There are very few people, even among those who are sick and poor, who cannot, if they will, count more comforts than serious deprivations, and with most people the comforts far outnumber the deprivations. With many, health seems the only thing lacking to a reasonable degree of joy and contentment. To work directly for the attainment of health or supply even by metaphysical means (and this is entirely legitimate, for a portion of one's activity), it is necessary to center thought in some measure on self and what self hopes to gain — and in some measure on the deprivation or lack which one seeks to overcome. On the other hand, to center the thought on God and on the comforts and blessings which one has — denying the sickness or lack in any given line as much as may be — and to lift the thought to God in gratitude for many comforts and blessings, is to take one's thought off self, and to place it on God, the universal good, thus tending to "overcome self," or to surrender self in spiritual love. Whoever will cultivate and attain this habitual recognition of God and gratitude to Him, will

Self-Surrender through Love

soon gain a quality of consciousness in which habitual sin, disease or poverty cannot continue. They will be overcome, not so much by direct effort as by crowding them out of experience through a general spiritualizing and uplifting of the consciousness of life. The direct effort is usually necessary, but it should always be supplemented by the indirect activity above described, an activity not really undertaken for the purpose of gaining any specific thing, but for both the duty and satisfaction of reflecting back to God that intelligence and love which He is constantly radiating toward man.

There are many cases of chronic disease which are yielding to direct effort through argument in Christian Science only slowly or seemingly, thus far, not at all, which will soon yield, if the direct effort is supplemented by self-surrender through habitual love and gratitude to God, ceasing to take the comforts and blessings of daily living as "matters of course" and thinking most of those things of which we seemed to be deprived, but following the suggestion of the Psalmist, so frequently repeated by him: "O, that men would praise the Lord for His goodness, and for His wonderful works to the children of men."

The ice which is upon the river or lake in midwinter did not form there in a day or a week, but represents the accumulation of the winter's cold. So a chronic disease, manifest in the body, did not get started there in a week or a month, but represents the *accumulation* of months or years of wrong thought and living. Could we turn upon the ice on the lake in midwinter the heat of a midsummer sun, we could cause it to break up and disappear in a very few days, but that is impossible. However, the *continued* shining of the sun of early spring, dispensing each day a comparatively slight amount of heat, *before very long* breaks up and melts away the ice. Could we turn upon the accumulation of wrong thought in mortal mind and the resulting disease a large realization of the love and power of God, and we often can, we could cause the disease to break up and wholly disappear in a few hours or days, and this is frequently done. But suppose we cannot command a sufficient realization to do this quickly, yet we can accomplish it *before very long*, if we persistently turn upon the evil condition even a small realization of God's love and power.

The first day that the spring sun shines, the ice is apparently not affected at all, nor the second day, nor for many days; but finally there comes a day when the ice is noticeably affected, even to the point of breaking in pieces. It was not alone that day's sunshine that accomplished this result, but the *accumulation* of the many days of shining that had gone before. So let us continue to cultivate spiritual thought by any and all methods, especially by love and gratitude to God, whether the disease seems to yield or not. If we do so persistently, not merely spasmodically, there will come a day when the disease will yield markedly, and this will be the result, not merely of the last days' spiritual work, but of the *accumulation* of our spiritual thought and growth. A wise man of the East has well said: "Let no man think lightly of good, saying in his heart, It will not come nigh unto me. Even by the falling of water drops a water pot is filled. So the wise man becomes full of good, even if he gathers it little by little. Even a good man sees evil days so long as his good [thoughts and] deeds do not ripen; but when his good [thoughts and] deeds ripen, then does the good man see good things."

MAKING THE PORT

A brave and skillful mariner, once well started on his voyage, never turns back, but keeps headed toward the port of his destination, no matter what obstacles present themselves. His ship, wisely steered and strongly propelled from within, makes progress even while it is being buffeted by the winds and waves. So shall I make progress, steered by the acknowledgment of God in all my ways, and propelled from within and above by Love and Truth. I will not truckle in spirit, nor yield for a moment my poise and self-control, nor even think of turning back in my course, because of pain, or any suggestions of doubt, fear, or despondency; but I shall win a victory over afflictions by patience, calmness, determination, perseverance, courage, and understanding, all born of God.

Just as the mariner does not ask the winds and waves whether or not he is making progress, but asks his chart and compass, so I will not ask the feelings or states of my body whether or not I am getting on, but I will ask my increasing understanding of God's word, which is my chart and compass. I will "look away from the body into Truth and Love." (*Science and Health*) I will, in my calculations of progress, "be absent from the body, and present with the Lord." And when this storm of distress passes, I shall be farther on than before it commenced, in moral strength, in character, in health, and in knowledge of the Truth.

When the storm arises, the mariner does not turn off steam and drift before the wind, anywhere it chooses to carry him; but he *turns on more steam* and keeps headed straight for port. So, when the storms of distress or suffering rise against me, I will not cease to know and declare Truth and Love, and I will not utter the complaints of mortal mind, and so let it carry me backward; but during the storm of suffering, I will hold on to Truth and Love all the harder.

I will declare them all the more stoutly. So shall I make progress toward final healing, even in the midst of the worst distress.

In the words of Paul, "Be not weary in well doing; for in due season you shall reap, if you faint not."

IS GOD OUR FATHER-MOTHER?

Is God our tender, loving Father-Mother? Potentially, yes — the Father-Mother of all men. But from a present, practical standpoint, whether He is our loving parent and provider depends upon us. Paul declares: "They which are the children of the flesh, these are not the children of God." Yet all human beings have the capacity to become the children of God. The fact is that we do not come naturally by a knowledge of God and of right relations with Him, any more than we come naturally by a knowledge of mathematics or music.

In so far as we gain a practical understanding of mathematics, we may be said to be children of mathematics, but this understanding has to be intelligently and laboriously acquired. Likewise, in so far as we diligently seek and acquire a knowledge of God and His law, and order our thoughts and lives in the continual consciousness of Him and in obedience to His law, in that far we are children of God; and He is our Father-Mother just so far as we thus become His children, and no farther. We get the benefit and care of divine Love just in proportion as we work our way into mental and practical accord with the law of divine Love.

It might be rather foolish for a man, confined in a dark cave, to claim that the sun was his source of light and heat; but if he could work his way out of the cave into the light, his claim would be justified. The sun does place light within the reasonable reach of every man in the world, but it will not chase a man into a cave or other dark place, as a dog follows its master, in order to give him light. The man must keep himself in the light which is within his reach. So God places all good within the reasonable reach of every man in the world, but God does not take separate account of every human being and follow each man into ignorance and sin, in such a way as to force knowledge and righteousness upon him without diligent effort on his own part. Each man must meet God half way. Paul declares that God is "a rewarder of them that *diligently* seek him."

What has just been stated may seem to be at variance with certain passages of Scripture. For instance, Jesus frequently declared: "The son of man is come to seek and save that which is lost." Undoubtedly Christ Jesus is God's representative in the world, but in a mediatorial capacity, such that the mediatorial Christ-mind, animating the activity of Jesus and other human beings, takes account of particular human needs in such a way as the absolute Mind, God, does not. Then Jesus declared concerning material food and rainment, "Your Heavenly Father knoweth that ye have need of these things." There seems little doubt that Jesus made this statement, as he did several others which are recorded in the New Testament, having in view the immature condition of the understanding of his auditors. He was feeding milk to the babes, rather than meat to strong men. So, instead of making some of his statements from the standpoint of absolute truth, he made them from the human viewpoint. When men "seek first the kingdom of God and His righteousness," as Jesus told them to do in this same connection, it does result that what they need materially is "added unto" them. It *works out* just as it would if God actually did know that they had need of these things, and took particular account of each man's need to supply it. Jesus declared: "God so loved the world, that He gave His only begotten son, that whosoever believeth on him, should not perish, but have everlasting life." This verse represents God as knowing of men who are lost, and as loving a lost world, and as deliberately sending His son into it. God's nature, as absolute perfection, would render this impossible; but since God is omnipresent good, and thus places all good, through His manifestations in the Christ, constantly in the reach of all men who are willing to seek diligently to appropriate what is thus provided, it works out in human experience *as though* God loved the world, and purposely sent His only begotten Son to be the Saviour of the world. "Beloved, now are we [who have been spiritually quickened] the sons of God, and it doth not yet appear what we shall be [when we have fully apprehended and demonstrated the divine sonship]; but we know that when He shall [fully] appear [to our advancing understanding], we shall be [shall then realize ourselves as being] like Him; for we shall see Him as He is."

THE LAME WALK

Be willing [choosing] to be absent [in thought] from the body, and to be present with the Lord.
           Paul

Look away from the body into Truth and Love, the Principle of all happiness, harmony, and immortality.
           Mary Baker Eddy

  Christ promised to his disciples in all ages: "He that believeth on me, the works that I do shall he do also." This same Christ declared, "I am the truth;" so his promise evidently means, He that understandeth me, the truth, and worketh from this basis of truth, the works that I do shall he do also. Jesus also declared that the knowledge of the truth should make men free from error and evil of various kinds. Evidently, therefore, the problem of being able to repeat the healing works of Jesus in these modern times is the problem of learning to understand and to apply the Christ-Truth.

  This Christ-Truth was taught and demonstrated by Jesus in Galilee, and was understood and practiced by his immediate disciples, and by his disciples of the first two or three centuries. Following that time, the understanding of the truth which makes it possible to heal the sick was lost, and remained for the most part unknown and unused until it was rediscovered from the Scriptures and again taught and demonstrated by the founder of the modern Christian Science movement, Mary Baker Eddy, who made her discovery in 1866, enlarged it in the years immediately following, and afterwards taught it to a rapidly increasing number of students, either through personal instruction, or through the Christian Science textbook, *Science and Health with Key to the Scriptures*, and through her other writings. Many of these students, through this instruction, have so learned to understand the Scriptures, that they are able in some measure to fulfill the commission of Christ, "Preach the gospel; heal the sick," in the same manner that he preached and healed.

As an exemplification that this is true, the author will speak of a few cases of healing which have been brought about under his own ministration, knowing, as he does, just what was done and said in order to effect the healing; and if he tells about them in considerable detail, it may serve to prove to some, who are just beginning to investigate Christian Science, the truth of the Principle and teachings of this Science; and it may help some to make demonstrations for themselves.

The writer was talking, one evening, with eight or ten laboring men, in a room where they were gathered; and, after a time, the conversation turned upon the subject of Christian Science. They began to ask questions, which the writer answered to the best of his ability, and which led up to other questions and answers — some of the answers given seeming quite strange and remarkable to some of the hearers. After a time, a young man sitting in a chair, with a crutch at each side, said, "If what you are saying is true, what about my ankle, here?" The writer asked, "What about your ankle?" Then the young man went on to relate that nearly a year before, while he was helping to handle some heavy telephone poles, one of them fell, by accident, upon his ankle and mashed it very badly. A surgeon removed more than a score of pieces of bone, and pieces of ligament, and bound up the ankle. Other pieces of bone festered out during following weeks. Then the skin healed over at the surface, but was red and of unnatural texture. The ankle was shrunken and remained so sore that it was impossible to touch the foot to the floor without excruciating pain. This condition had continued for many months, and no improvement was evident; and the young man had been obliged to walk with two crutches ever since the accident, and his physicians could not seem to do anything for him. Other men in the group, who were well acquainted with the young man, confirmed the account. After listening to his story, he writer took up a Socratic line of questioning, and led the young man to assent to the following propositions, which will be seen to be logically related to each other:

God is Spirit. God is infinite intelligence, infinite Love, and infinite will. Intelligence, feeling, and will are the characteristics of Mind, and since God manifests all these in infinite degree, He is infinite Mind; that is, infinite Mind is God; and Spirit is infinite Mind; so these are interchangeable names for the Deity.

God is sole Creator, as the Scripture teaches. Therefore, infinite Mind is sole Creator. On stopping to think about it, we perceive that the creations of Mind are necessarily mental, that is to say, ideas. Therefore, all that is created by the sole Creator consists of ideas, which are true, changeless, eternal, and perfect or harmonious, according to the nature of Mind, God, who thinks them into being.

Ideas are either simple or compound. Let us illustrate. The multiplication table is a compound idea, made up of simpler ideas, like the ideas, "two times three equals six," "four times five equals twenty," and so on. Some of the ideas which constitute the real universe are compound ideas, and other ideas are simpler ideas included within these compound ideas.

If you are anything at all, God made you; for God makes all that is made. If God made you, you are the creation of infinite Mind; and so you are the idea of God, in His image and likeness, and you are not a form of matter, whatever the appearance may be. You are the compound idea of God, and every part of you, known as it is, is a simpler idea of God, included in the compound idea, which you are. Before proceeding farther to the particular point which we are to make, in order that we may understand it more clearly when made, let us examine in a little detail the nature of an idea. Let us take one that we are familiar with, the idea, "two times three equals six." There never was a time when it was not true, when it was not a fact or an actuality, that two times three equals six; there never will be a time when it will not be a fact or an actuality; there is not a place in the universe where it is not now a fact or an actuality. So that idea is as enduring as eternity, and as large as the universe, like the infinite creative Mind, which ordained this idea as true and real. You will readily see that this idea cannot be improved, for it is already perfect of its kind; and it cannot be impaired, for nothing has power over it, save God alone, who ordained it as eternally true. It cannot be destroyed. As is true of God Himself, "from everlasting to everlasting" two times three equals six. All God's ideas, all His creations, are endowed with His changelessness, indestructibleness, and perfection.

Can you conceive of anyone changing the idea "two times three equals six?" Could anyone bury it? Could anyone lock it up? Could anyone run it through a machine and mangle it? Could a telephone pole fall on it and crush it? Evidently not; for the idea "two times three equals six" is infinite and omnipresent, and is not in or of matter, nor subject to the power of matter. Material symbols of this idea may be made with chalk upon the blackboard, or with the pencil on paper; but the idea is not in those symbols, nor in any way governed by them, though it may be expressed by them into mortal men. Whatever may happen to the symbols does not at all happen to the idea; for the idea is ever the same.

If you have any ankle, God made it; that is, infinite Mind thought it into being, and holds it in being as an everlasting and true idea; and like the Mind which thinks and holds it in being, this idea is infinite, omnipresent, unpicturable, without outlines, changeless, and perfect. It is neither in matter nor composed of matter. Therefore, your ankle, the ankle which God made, which is the only ankle there is (for there is no other Creator), was never under a telephone pole, and never could have been crushed by one. What you call your ankle is but an unreal material symbol of some real idea, or rather, a false concept thereof. If now we know and declare the truth, the fact, about your real ankle as we have just done, this knowledge of the truth will destroy the belief of discord, pain, and weakness in connection with that belief which seems to you to be your ankle. In other words, this knowledge and declaration of the truth will cause the unreal symbol to appear harmonious instead of discordant. I tell you, the only real ankle you have, the ankle which God made, the divine and perfect idea ankle, was never under a telephone pole and was never crushed; and any false appearances in connection with that which seems to be your ankle have no reality, and no power to remain; for they are mere false beliefs, lies of Satan, which the truth that we have just declared has power to correct, and so destroy.

Within three days, without anything further being done or said, the young man hung up his crutches and began to walk about with a light cane. The soreness and weakness had almost entirely disappeared. A short time later, he discarded the cane also. Within a few weeks of the time of the conversation, he was acting as conductor on an open street car, making his way on and off the car, and along the running-boards filled with standing men, with as much ease as though no accident had ever happened to him. In truth, it never did, although it so appeared in the realm of mortal belief. But our Lord and Savior said: "Judge not by appearances, but judge righteous judgment," which righteous judgment we did judge, in connection with the young man's ankle.

The writer presumes that this account may seem strange doctrine to some who have not made a study of Christian Science; but he wishes to call attention to the following fact: He told that young man that his real ankle, the only ankle he actually had, was an idea of God, boundless, eternal, indestructible, and perfect; and that his real ankle was never under a telephone pole, and was never crushed. When he made that statement to him, he told him either the truth, or a falsehood. It was one or the other. The statement did more for the young man within a few days than skillful physicians, aided by the so-called healing forces of nature, had been able to do for him in many months. You do not believe that a falsehood would have such healing power. If the statement was not a falsehood, it was a truth; and it is a truth which illustrates the nature of all reality. The whole real universe is an ideal universe, consisting of divine ideas, which are eternally and changelessly endowed with the harmony, perfection, beauty, and uprightness of God, their Maker. And whoever knows this fact, and will maintain it in his thinking, and declare it when there is occasion, can, according to the measure and clearness of his understanding and realization, overcome the discords, diseases, and troubles with which he seems to be afflicted; and, in greater or lesser measure, he can perform a like service for his fellow men.

To avoid possibility of misconception, let it be clearly stated that the divine ideas, of which the ankle, heart, eyes, and other parts and organs of the human body are reversed counterfeits or misconceptions, are all limitless, unpicturable, without shape, and their precise nature and office in Mind "doth not yet appear," but will appear as we come to understand God more fully. As God does not use articulate speech, these divine ideas are, of course, not known to divine Mind by the names given by men to their mortal counterfeits. The real body is the body or sum-total of right ideas, completely expressing God. The teaching of this article is not an attempt at spiritualizing matter or the human body. On the other hand, it advocates "replacing the objects of material sense with spiritual ideas." (*Science and Health*) It is not an attempt at localizing these ideas, but teaches their boundlessness and omnipresence.

Christian Science is pure metaphysics; that is, it is above, beyond, and over physics, or that which is visible and material. In the experience of any student at the start, Christian Science does not correspond at all to the so-called physical or sensible world; yet it is true, that, if a student will study and accept Christian Science as a purely mental or metaphysical science, when he is firmly established on its metaphysical basis, he can then use his knowledge to produce visible changes in the so-called physical realm. Archimedes, when he discovered the basic law of leverage said, "Give me where to stand [outside the world], and I will move the world." Christian Science does give us a firm mental standing-ground outside the so-called physical and visible; and, having discovered and learned to stand upon this basis, according to the measure and absoluteness of our metaphysical realization, we can move off the physical appearances named diseases, whether organic or inorganic, so-called. With a very complete and absolute realization of the metaphysical, we could produce even more marvelous changes in the so-called physical. Jesus was the master metaphysician of all who have ever appeared upon the earth; and he, from the metaphysical standpoint, not only healed all manner of disease, but changed the water into wine, multiplied the loaves and fishes, caused the fig tree to wither to the roots, restored the withered hand, gave sight to the blind, hearing to the deaf, and caused the lame to walk.

As confirmatory evidence that the method of work above described is efficacious, and that it is actually workable in daily practice, the author will speak very much more briefly of two or three other cases of healing.

A lady complained of having a large number of corns on her toes, which had caused her much annoyance for many years. The writer took up a line of thought with her, just as he did with the young man, and showed her that her real toes are ideas of God eternal, changeless, and perfect. He also showed her that just as the simpler ideas of the multiplication table abide together within the table, and never get in each other's way or interfere with each other, likewise our real toes, as ideas of God, eternally dwell together in creative Mind, and never get in each other's way, or interfere with each other, nor can they be made to do so. He said to her that she seemed to have trouble with her toes because she believed the false sense about them, and thought them to be material, limited, and subject to change and disease; and he showed her that this could not be true of anything which God created, and He made all that is made. Following this conversation, without further treatment the lady forgot about her feet, until chancing to look at them a few days later, she found no corns in evidence, although the trouble had seemed to be a fixed condition for years. A false declaration could not have cured her so remarkably; so the declaration was true, and illustrates the ideality and changeless perfection of the real universe, and the real man.

A lady showed the author a hand badly broken out in appearance with what is called salt-rheum, which condition had been in evidence several weeks. She knew nothing of Christian Science. So, without preliminary explanation, the writer declared to her directly that her hand was an idea of God, an idea in Mind, and not a form of matter; that her real blood was the same as the blood of Christ — namely, divine Life and Love (the writer was not referring to the blood of Jesus, which was the same as that of any other mortal, but to the blood of Christ); and so her real blood could not be impure; that the substance of her hand was creative Mind, which eternally upholds the idea which her hand is; and so neither her hand, nor its substance, nor its blood, could, in truth, be diseased. Nothing else was said; but she left the room and forgot about the hand, until, chancing to look at it next morning, she found it whole and fair like the other.

These demonstrations are among thousands made by Christian Science practitioners, which give visible proof of the significance and truth of the following words of Mrs. Eddy: "Every creation or idea of Spirit has its counterfeit in some matter-belief. Every material belief hints the existence of spiritual reality; and if mortals are instructed in spiritual things, it will be seen that material belief, in all its manifestations, reversed, will be found the type and representative of verities priceless, eternal, and just at hand." (*Miscellaneous Writings*)

The writer was most remarkably healed through the demonstration of Christian Science, and has been blessed in countless ways in his own personal experience; and for these blessings, and for the understanding of the Scriptures which has enabled him to be of some help to his fellow men, he gives thanks to God and the Lord Jesus, and he also gratefully remembers the woman through whose discovery, labors, and sacrifices this healing truth has been made known to this age and generation — Mary Baker Eddy.

ABOUT THE AUTHOR: *Dominion Within* has a very interesting history. Soon after Mrs. Eddy's passing — and in direct defiance of her admonitions — the Christian Science Board of Directors began the policy of "unauthorized literature," wherein no Church member could circulate or publish any work on Christian Science without the Directors' approval. It was this policy that led Rev. Kratzer to publish his book.

Glenn A. Kratzer was born in 1869. There is no record of his place of birth or his early years. He was a Protestant Minister before coming into Christian Science in 1906. He had Primary Class instruction with Edward A. Kimball, C.S.D. and in 1908 he and his wife Elizabeth became Christian Science practitioners listed in *The Christian Science Journal*.

Rev. Kratzer apparently did outstanding healing work, for patients came to him from all parts of the country. From the year he found Christian Science, his articles were published in the periodicals.

Rev. Kratzer and his wife, Elizabeth, were living in Chicago when they went into the practice. After attending First Church, Chicago, for three years, he applied for membership. In December, 1912, when interviewed by the Board of the Church, he was asked if he was giving his own manuscripts to patients to study, and if he was teaching them. When he said he did both, he was not recommended for membership.

In February, 1913, he received a letter from John Dittemore, secretary of The Mother Church, informing him that information had reached the Directors to the effect that he was furnishing patients with his own "written formulas and articles in preferences to the literature provided by our Leader and our Publishing Society." Rev. Kratzer was charged with disobedience to the By-laws in the *Church Manual*. and was given a "blank form of request for dismissal" to sign and return to the Directors.

Rev. Kratzer wrote, explaining that he did not furnish patients with his own writings in preference to Mrs. Eddy's and those of the Publishing Society. His patients owned *Science and Health* and most subscribed to the periodicals. His writings were merely to help patients remember what he had told them relevant to their needs. He did sign and return the "blank form for dismissal," and his name was immediately dropped from the *Journal* and Church membership.

After leaving The Mother Church, Rev. Kratzer apparently continued as a practitioner. He soon thereafter published *Dominion Within*. This was followed by the publication of several other books, including his compilation of his teacher's addresses and notes from classes, which became the classic book, *Teaching and Addresses of Edward A. Kimball, C.S.D.*

In an effort to explain his reasons for sharing his articles with patients, Rev. Kratzer wrote the following letter to the Directors:

717 Oakwood Blvd.,
Chicago, Ill.

To The Directors of The First Church of Christ, Scientist,
Boston, Massachusetts.

Gentlemen:-

I am credibly informed, though not directly or officially, that charges are to be filed against me with your Board, either by a practitioner of Chicago, or by the Board of First Church of Chicago, if said practitioner can induce said Board to take such action. I recently applied for membership in First Church, and its Board refused to recommend my name for membership to the Church. In the examination before the Board, practically the same matters were discussed which, I understand, are to be made the basis of the charges, if they are preferred against me.

The matters at issue seem to be somewhat as follows: I am accused of "teaching" my patients "psychology," of a nature contrary to Christian Science; of "teaching" my patients without authorization, and for improper compensation; and of using my own papers and other "unauthorized" literature in my practice.

As to my authorization to teach my patients, I would speak first of Mrs. Eddy's often quoted direction in Miscellaneous Writings, "Teach by healing, and heal by teaching." At the bottom of page 417, of Science and Health, Mrs. Eddy gives direction to the practitioner: "Explain audibly to your patients, as soon as they can bear it, the complete control which Mind holds over the body. Show them how mortal mind seems to induce disease by certain fears and false conclusions, and how divine Mind can cure by opposite thoughts. Give your patients an underlying understanding to support them and to shield them from the baneful effects of their own conclusions." There is nothing to indicate that this direction was given only to so-called "authorized teachers", and that it was not a direction for all practitioners, even for those whose names are not in the *Journal*. These words, it seems to me, are sufficient warrant for a practitioner to explain to his patients any phase of truth that he thinks will help the patient, or to uncover to the patient any of the hidden ways of error. A great deal of experience in the practice has shown me that such explanation and uncovering often greatly facilitates the healing of the patient; but, to do this, requires far more of a practitioner's time than to merely make a few desultory remarks to a patient, and then give him silent treatment. Accordingly, it is but fair and just that the patient should pay according to the time spent, and it is my custom to charge at the rate of two dollars per hour for my time in explaining Science audibly and in the treatment that follows. Absent treatments, I give at the rate of one dollar each. These rates are certainly not higher than those of reputable physicians practicing in this City.

I have had many calls to treat people in various parts of the country. It has always been so since I took up the practice. Many of my patients have been students of Science for from two to ten or fifteen years. Many of them have previously had several practitioners. Many of them write and ask me questions about various phases of Science, saying that they have been unable to find anything in their reading which made this matter plain to them. Sometimes they say that they believe that if this particular point could be made clear to them, they would be able to work more effectually for themselves, and that their healing would be promoted. It has been my custom to dictate answers to all such questions, in the form of articles rather than in the form of letters. Carbon copies of these articles I have kept and placed on file in alphabetical order. If, later on, some other patient should ask the same question, I would send or hand that patient an article which had previously been prepared to meet this need for another, as representing the most mature and carefully considered answer which I have been able to give.

All the articles that I ever sent in for publication were written under exactly these circumstances. I never yet wrote an article for the sake of writing an article. All have been written primarily to help patients whom I was treating. My article, 'Dominion Within' concerning which Mrs. Eddy wrote me "Your article, 'Dominion Within' is superb," was written for a patient in Chicago when I was living in Fitchburg.

A pertinent question is, Should the By-laws of the Mother Church be interpreted as legitimately suppressing, in all cases, such activity on the part of the practitioner? This question I wish to discuss fully. On the right answer to it, hang great issues to the future of Science.

Were Jesus to reappear among us, today, he could not perform his office as a member of the Christian Science church. He would not be allowed to speak in public, nor would he be allowed to write and publish, as he would undoubtedly do, if he were to attempt a ministry to this age where papers and books are in such common use.

All through human history, the tendency of religious movements has been to center thought more and more about man-made rules, about forms and ceremonies, about buildings and outward display, and to center it less and less upon spontaneous spiritual activity upon the part of the members. This tendency is very noticeable in the Christian Science organization, even in the first half century of its existence. "If they do these things in the green tree, what will they do in the dry?"

It is very important to preserve purity of doctrine among Christian Scientists, yet it is equally important to preserve liberty of expression. "Where the Spirit of the Lord is, there is liberty." For Christian Science Boards of Directors to say, We are going to preserve purity of doctrine among the people at any cost, no matter whether individual liberty of expression be stifled or not, will result in forcing many of the people into a one-sided development, very much to their harm, and, ultimately, very much to the harm of the organization itself. The history of human experience has shown that the human race has had quite as hard a struggle to gain liberty for the rank and file of the people as it has had to gain knowledge of the truth; and the great body of Christian Scientists are quite as much in danger of losing their God-given liberties of expression as they are of losing correct understanding; and one loss is just as dangerous as the other, either to the individual, or to the organization as a whole in the long account.

On the subject of literature, the *Manual of the Mother Church* undoubtedly takes exactly the right stand, in prescribing that "A member of this Church shall neither buy, sell, nor circulate Christian Science literature which is not correct in its statements of the divine Principle and rules and the demonstration of Christian Science." This places the standard of judgment and discrimination where it ought to be placed, — namely, with truth, Christ. But to make a rule that a Christian Scientist shall not circulate literature unless it bears the stamp of a certain human institution, is to attempt to establish "traditions of men, after the rudiments of the world, and not after Christ."

Undoubtedly, so-called "authorized literature" is more likely to be correct in doctrine than literature which has not been officially revised; and, no doubt, a great body of authorized literature is very important. And if this literature continues to be published and circulated, as at present, it will serve as a standard of correct doctrine among students of Christian Science. If some of them do pick up a false idea here and there, they will in time discover its falsity, through their reading and study of the authorized literature. As long as the authorized literature continues to be issued, as at present, the Christian Science movement will be like a running stream, constantly tending to purify itself, even though some impurities do get into it through the circulation of unauthorized literature. Whatever might be lost through temporary and occasional corruption of doctrine would be more than compensated for, if members of the church are allowed freedom in speech and writing, by the fresh, spiritual life, direct from God, that will be energizing the activity of members of the church, here and there. *Only* through the encouragement of such liberty of expression can the *spiritual* life of the Christian Science organization be permanently maintained. From a spiritual standpoint, it is absolutely unsafe, in the long account, to force, or attempt to force, all of the members of the church on to a Procrustean bed of uniformity, as to their activities in speech and writing. In the preface to *Science and Health*, Mrs. Eddy declares: "The time for thinkers has come". Woe to the Christian Science organization, if through over strict adherence to its By-laws, it stifles the activity of its thinkers. The authorities of the organization need to heed the scriptural warning about stoning the prophets.

As it seems to me, men are not for By-laws, but By-laws for men. Hence, By-laws should not be slavishly obeyed, but should be simply regarded as general rules, to be often set aside in special cases. They should be interpreted, not in the light of blind obedience, but in the light of common sense. Which member of your Board strictly obeys Article VIII, Section 12, which reads: "A member of the Church shall not patronize a publishing house or book store that has for sale obnoxious books." If any of you trade at almost any book store in your city, you are trading at a store which has on sale all forms of mental science books and books which attack Christian Science in the most virulent manner. You interpret that By-law in the light of common sense. You judge for yourself, whether you ought to obey that By-law or not. I have an equal right to judge for myself what literature I will use in connection with my practice in Christian Science, and I cannot justly be adjudged guilty of misconduct, in the sight of God, if I do not give out false teaching, whether or not what I give out has been "authorized." If I am not guilty in the sight of God, there is no just ground of excluding me from any church that bears the name of Christ. There is no utterance in sacred literature that needs more to be heeded by any religious organization that would perpetuate its spiritual life than Paul's exclamation: "Woe is me, if I preach not the gospel"; and no organization can safely abridge that impulse on the part of its members for any great length of time. When religious life ceases to be spontaneous, it ceases to be true religion at all, and degenerates into mere formalism.

Mrs. Eddy's thought of the ultimate right condition for Christian Scientists is clearly brought out in the following quotations from her writings:

From *Retrospection and Introspection*: "Despite the prosperity of my church, it was learned that material organization has its value and peril, and that organization is requisite only in the earliest periods in Christian history. After this material form of cohesion and fellowship has accomplished its end, continued organization retards spiritual growth, and should be laid off, — even as the corporeal organization deemed requisite in the first stages of mortal existence is finally laid off, in order to gain spiritual freedom and supremacy." (Page 45. Page 64 in editions earlier than 1910.)

In *Miscellaneous Writings*, she says, "When students have fulfilled all the good ends of organization and are convinced that by leaving the material forms thereof a higher spiritual unity is won, then is the time to follow the example of the *Alma Mater*. Material organization is requisite in the beginning; but when it has done its work, the purely Christly method of teaching and preaching must be adopted. . . . Growth is restricted by forcing humanity out of the proper channels for development, or by holding it in fetters." (Pages 358, 359.)

I think that Mrs. Eddy was inspired when she wrote these words just quoted. They are of the same import as those of St. John in the 13th chapter of Revelation, whose words were also inspired. If Mrs. Eddy was inspired when she wrote the By-laws, and when she selected Directors for the Mother Church, is there any reason why she was not as much inspired when she wrote the words just quoted.

The question at issue in my thought concerns freedom of speech and freedom of the press as related to the By-laws and their administration and enforcement by the Christian Science Board of Directors.

I do not assert that the time has yet arrived when entire liberty of public utterance should be given to all Scientists. It seems to me that the time is rapidly approaching, if not at hand. However, the precise time is not the question at issue. The precise question in my thought I will state in the next paragraph.

Mrs. Eddy is gone from among us, in the human sense. She has left the Christian Science Organization to be governed by a certain set of By-laws, printed in a *Manual*. One of the provisions of this Manual is; "This Manual shall not be revised without the written consent of its author." That means, that unless Mrs. Eddy is resurrected, the By-laws can never be legally changed. I freely admit that the Directors are not responsible for making them, nor have they any authority to change them. I do not believe that, had Mrs. Eddy suspected that she would pass on at the time she did, some years before it happened, or even a few weeks before it happened, she would have left matters in that situation.

She has gone away and left the infant organization pinned up in swaddling clothes. Anybody can see that these must be unpinned, sooner or later. Who is to do it? And when? Are there any plans with regard to this? Or is it the unquestioned thought at headquarters that the present state of affairs should continue indefinitely?

We all hope that the civilized world will soon embrace Christian Science. We hope that it may have the benefits which can accrue from constructive organization. But that the speaking and writing of the civilized world on the subject of religion should be under the supervision of five men in Boston, and largely subject to suppression by them, is unthinkable. If it were thinkable, it would be "unspeakable."

Your Board of Directors is self-perpetuating. As I understand it, if one of you should resign, the other four would elect his successor. In any case, your Board is to continue, having absolute authority as to the appointment of lecturers, and suppressing all other speakers, making provision for the appointment of teachers, and exercising a vast influence as to what shall be published and what shall not be published. Now, you have read enough of human history to know that all human organizations, especially those of an autocratic nature, have a tendency to magnify their own importance, as years and centuries go by, and to reach out for more and more authority and control, by the unwritten law of custom, if not by the written law. Granted that those of you now in power would do nothing of the kind, relatively speaking, the time is not far distant when you must have successors. Through the tendencies to conservatism and to the worship of organization in human nature, I can see an imminent danger that the Christian Science hierarchy, if allowed to proceed unquestioned, will soon become so entrenched in its own sense of authority and in the blind support of the comparatively unthinking masses of Scientists and others, that it will get a "strangle hold" on the mental liberties of a large section of the civilized world; and to enslave men mentally, — that is, to impede their freedom of mental action and utterance, — is far more damnable than to enslave them physically. How long will it be before we shall have an "index expurgatorious"?

There is only one way that I can see, in which the threatened danger can be averted. That is, for such Christian Scientists as wish to do so, to exercise their God-given and (American) constitutional liberties of freedom of speech and freedom of the press on the subject of Christian Science. It seems to me that if the Directors are wise, they will omit to enforce the By-laws against the Scientists who do so, except in cases where liberty of expression is being very unwisely used; and will omit to enforce such By-laws more and more; and gradually suffer them to relapse into "innocuous desustude," like the "Blue laws" of New England, which are still on the Statute books, though not enforced.

As a beginning, if the Directors would countenance and not discourage those who write and speak according to Principle, — whose utterances are scientifically correct, namely for the present doing what they can to suppress unscientific presentations, it would, as it seems to me, mark great progress.

At the present time, I know of two or three people of great prominence and capabilities who are much interested in Science, and are likely to become Scientists in doctrine, but I doubt if they will ever join the organization so long as their liberty of expression is likely to be interfered with. There are going to be more and more such people attracted to the scientific understanding. Why would it not be well to have such a policy that we can number them among us and turn their talents to us?

Christian Science is an exact science. Why should it not be taught by any person or institution who cares to teach it just as freely as mathematics? I expect to live to see the day when many of our universities will wish to establish chairs of Christian Science. Why should they not be allowed to do so? I am inclined to think that before long some of them will, whether they are "allowed or not."

We need a central organization to publish our periodicals and literature, to appoint authorized lecturers and teachers, and to do other constructive work; but it does seem to me that we no longer need an organization to suppress anybody. With authorized publications, teachers, and lecturers, firmly established as they now are, there is no doubt that the strain of scientific knowledge would be kept pure by those standards, no matter how many should speak, teach and write on their own initiative. If some get "off the track" doctrinally for a time, through the established standards they would in time get back. In any case as the situation now is, the danger of false doctrine does not seem nearly as great as the danger of tyranny. The "keeping-the-Science-pure" idea is likely to become the chief instrument of tyranny. Already as it seems to me, the vast majority of Christian Scientists have become mesmerized with the idea, so that it is disproportionately emphasized, to the neglect or suppression of other things fully as important. To allow the Scientists liberty of the Spirit is even more important than purity of the letter is.

You see, it is no mere personal question that I am raising. If it were a mere personal affair, I could get along with it better; but it is a question of vast importance to humanity. In considering that question, please do not take into consideration my personal problem at all, as that would not influence me in the least. To show me what is the prudent thing from a personal standpoint, will not help me at all. When it comes to a question of liberty — especially the liberties of mankind, — I consider my personal health, prosperity, or human life, as dust in the balance. If I know that it is the right thing for me to assess my liberties in this direction, I would do it, even though I were crucified for it.

I see grave danger threatening the Christian Science movement, its human side, and I must not fail to give warning. This letter is intended, in all loving kindness, to uncover the error that threatens, and to make plain its more or less hidden ways.

Any student of the history of the religious development of mankind knows that one of the worst tendencies of the human mind is to multiply man-made laws and rules as a test of conformity and righteousness in religion. To the Jews were originally given the so-called laws of Moses, which were embodied in their sacred literature, the heart of which were the Ten Commandments. Not satisfied with these laws, the authorities of the Jewish Church made interpretations of these laws, which interpretations soon acquired a supposed sanctity through continued usage, and became as binding upon the activities of the people as the original laws. This sort of thing went on, until, in the time of Jesus, such interpretations as the following concerning the commandment against breaking the Sabbath were in force:

"A member of the Jewish Church must not wear sandals with nails in them on the Sabbath since by doing so he would be carrying unnecessary weight, and so performing unnecessary labor, on the Sabbath.

"In leading a beast to water on the Sabbath, the halter stale must be kept tight, to avoid bearing unnecessary weight through letting it sag, and thus violating the Sabbath."

Any member of the Jewish Church who violated such rules as these was as liable to discipline or expulsion as though he had broken one of the original Ten Commandments.

The mortal or carnal mind does not change very much with the lapse of centuries, and if Christian Science Boards of Directors go on making rules and interpretations of laws at the rate they are now doing in some of the branch churches, it will not be a hundred years till regulations as foolish as the above will be in force in Christian Science churches. The nature of mortal mind is such, that a church rule, designed to meet a special emergency, acquires sanctity in the minds of the people by usage and remains in force long after the special emergency which called the rule into formation has passed away and been forgotten. A rule, once made, and enforced for a number of years, it often takes nothing less than a revolution to break people loose from its shackles; and human rules are so very apt to be perverted from the purpose intended.

The essential error of Romanism is its practice of teaching the people to take their authority as to doctrine and practice from a man, a hierarchy, and a human organization, rather than from God. Man-rule, man-authority, is the crying sin of Catholicism. How could the Catholic Church fall into such an error? Simply because such a disposition is inherent in the carnal mind, and finds expression in the Catholic organization. Christian Scientists are far from having eliminated the carnal mind from their midst and from their activities, and carnal mind among Christian Scientists is identical with what is among Romanists, and unless watched and eliminated, will lead them into precisely the same errors.

Already, the Catholic "Index Expurgatorius" (A list of forbidden books) is duplicated among Christian Scientists by the official ban against "unauthorized literature." A sentiment is rapidly growing up among Christian Scientists, with regard to Mrs. Eddy, which, if not checked, will, with fifty or a hundred years, parallel "the Virgin Mary" worship among Catholics. The intolerable mental and spiritual tyranny exercised by the Roman hierarchy over the thinkers, the so-called "modernists" among the members of the Roman Church, is rapidly finding duplication in the ecclesiastical tyranny being exercised by the Christian Science organization, through its officials, against the liberty of speech and of press among its members, for which our revolutionary forefathers fought and died, and to attain which, in the history of the race, a thousand battlefields have been drenched with human blood. Liberties gained at such a price are not lightly to be thrown away.

For myself, I wish to say, and reiterate, that I have no desire to injure the Cause of Christian Science in any way, or to create discord. To give a man of my temperament, training, and habits, the glorious truth, and then require him to go on year after year without any public utterance in the way of speaking, and only semi-occasionally in the way of writing, is a hard position, — how hard I think those who have not had a minister's training and experience can hardly appreciate. It is good deal like placing a duck to live beside a pond of water, and require him to stay all the time on land.

I am not aware that, in my practice of Christian Science, I have habitually violated any other By-laws of the Mother Church; and if I have violated any of them in any particular instances, it has been by inadvertence or through some mere technicality, where I have not violated them in spirit. I have not circulated any literature that the *Manual of the Mother Church* forbids me to circulate. However, in my practice, I have frequently and habitually violated some of the established customs, and some of the suggestions that have been given out from headquarters. Ways in which I have done so, I have set forth in this letter, and with my reasons for doing so, which, on careful consideration, I hope and believe your Board will consider to be adequate.

On page 50, of *Retrospection and Introspection*, Mrs. Eddy says: "By loyalty in students, I mean this, — allegiance to God, subordination of the human to the divine, steadfast justice, and strict adherence to divine Truth and Love." While my personal conduct may not have been always irreproachable, — and what human beings' conduct has, — I feel that, as measured by our Leader's own definition, my loyalty, — at least in desire and purpose, — to the Cause of Christian Science cannot legitimately be doubted; and I feel that there should continue to be a place for me in the Christian Science organization, — and that without the imputation of "disloyalty."

I shall not consider it a discourtesy, if your Board does not deem it wise to reply to this letter, beyond acknowledging its receipt.

Very lovingly and loyally yours,
(Signed) G. A. Kratzer

After leaving The Mother Church, Rev. Kratzer wrote the following to a friend:

Dear Brother, you still do not understand me, and I want you to if possible, for you are one of my dearest friends. In your letter you say, "At that time (i.e. previous to leaving Springfield) your articles were appearing not infrequently, and you commanded the confidence and large expectations of all." If I was working for the "confidence" or praise of men, this should have satisfied me, but I wasn't. I never have since I have been in Science. The motive was strong in me in my early life; but in the ministry I had to stand in my pulpit and tell men of their worst faults, so that they knew just who I meant, and were not laboring under the misapprehension that I was talking about the faults of the Jews. I had to do this, and did it too many times not to have crucified the natural desire for the praise of men. I have always been controlled to some degree by the desire to enlighten men with the truth, to help men, but even that is not fundamental, and has not been for years. I am going to see if I can make language convey to you what is fundamental in me with regard to my activities in speech and writing; and if you can understand my case, I think you can then understand (if you do not already) why all clergymen find it so hard to work in the Christian Science organization.

During the first years of a man's ministry, the production of two sermons per week taxes his powers to the utmost. It is not joyful or spontaneous labor, by any means, but is often comparable in irksomeness to the school boy's writing compositions. But if a clergyman keeps at it long enough, he gradually acquires what ministers speak of as "Fertility of Mind," such that every sermon he works out suggests three or four more, and it is no longer a question of what he shall preach about, but what of the over-flowing abundance of ideas that come to him, he shall reject in favor of others that seem better. After a man has once come into this experience, he is a changed man, and is no more like his former self, and no more like the vast majority of men and women in this particular respect than an oak is like the acorn from which it sprang. If the oak were sentient, one might present to it numerous and weighty reasons why it should return into the acorn stage; but, however weighty the reasons that might be given, the oak simply could not do it. There are not reasons enough in the universe to make it possible for a mind that has acquired fertility of expression to behave like one that has not, no matter what reasons may be given why it would be wise to do so. A minister of the true type, working in Christian Science, simply cannot work within the circumscribed lines that an ordinary practitioner works in easily and naturally; for the ordinary practitioner has never gone through the years of labor that ultimate in fertility of thought and expression. Those who have not had this experience find it very difficult to understand this activity of the comparatively few who have.

You speak of the fact that my articles were appearing occasionally in the periodicals. How much does the appearing of a dozen articles a year amount to, as a means of expression, to a man whose mentality is so fertile that it would naturally produce an article every day? How would it seem to Paderewski, if someone should say to him, "You ought to be satisfied is you are allowed to give a dozen concerts a year." I think that you and I can readily imagine about what kind of a reply Paderewski would make. A man like Paderewski plays, not primarily "to be heard of men," not even primarily to entertain or elevate men, but primarily because he is so full of music; and to inhibit the musical expression of such a man would be to strike at his very life. And it would not help him a particle to tell him that, for certain reasons, it was inexpedient that he should be allowed much musical expression, but that he could express himself in painting all he cared to, — in fact, that it would be very useful if he would do so. Likewise, activity in healing the sick does not provide a proper outlet for a mentality fertilized in speaking and writing. There is really not a position in the Christian Science movement that provides an outlet for a highly fertilized mentality, except editorship of the periodicals, or Publication Committee work. A lectureship would answer the purpose in some measure, — fully so, if the lecturer were free to give *different* lectures practically every time he spoke, — not being confined to practically one lecture that had been written and submitted to the Board of Directors for approval. The position of a teacher would provide such an outlet, if a man were free to teach as often as pupils came to him. But the work of an ordinary practitioner, along ordinary lines, provides as adequate a means of expression for a fertilized mentality as painting would for one gifted and trained in music.

Although a man like Paderewski would not and could not play for any other primary reason than that he was full of music and must play, yet he could not express himself satisfactorily without an audience of one or more. Likewise, a spiritually fertilized mentality, though it does not express itself primarily for the sake of men, cannot rightly express itself, either in speech or writing, without an audience or one or more, — without someone with a view to whom the expression is made. For one to attempt to express himself in speech or writing without an audience of one, or without publication in view, would be to engage in action apart from its natural and legitimate purpose, which is a monstrosity in nature and is destructive to health and happiness. It may *now* be plain why I cannot write articles and then suppress their use, — with my patients at least, if there is no larger a field of expression. To do so would be to abuse the divine Spirit in me, and, as it seems to me, there can be no sufficient reason for me to do that.

Since I have been in the Science movement, I have felt much as a business man would who, with an investment of a hundred thousand dollars capitol, should, for eight years, do about a five thousand dollar business. He would feel that his capital was largely going to waste, and I have felt that my developed energies were largely going to waste, when they might have been giving splendid service, if I had been permitted to use them freely in the service of the Truth which I love.

G. A. Kratzer
Chicago, April 2nd, 1913

For further information regarding Christian Science:
Write: The Bookmark
Post Office Box 801143
Santa Clarita, CA 91380
Call: 1-800-220-7767
Visit our website: www.thebookmark.com